# HOW TO TALK TO ANYONE AT WORK

AVOID AWKWARDNESS, BANISH SOCIAL ANXIETY,
AND ACHIEVE YOUR GREATEST PROFESSIONAL
GOALS WITHOUT ACTING FAKE

CARL WOLFE

© **Copyright 2023 - All rights reserved.**

The content contained within this book may not be reproduced, duplicated, or transmitted without direct written permission from the author or the publisher.

Under no circumstances will any blame or legal responsibility be held against the publisher, or author, for any damages, reparation, or monetary loss due to the information contained within this book, either directly or indirectly.

Legal Notice:

This book is copyright protected. It is only for personal use. You cannot amend, distribute, sell, use, quote, or paraphrase any par, or the content within this book, without the consent of the author or publisher.

Disclaimer Notice:

Please note the information contained within this document is for educational and entertainment purposes only. All effort has been executed to present accurate, up-to-date, reliable, and complete information. No warranties of any kind are declared or implied. Readers acknowledge that the author is not engaged in the rendering of legal, financial, medical, or professional advice. The content within this book has been derived from various sources. Please consult a licensed professional before attempting any techniques outlined in this book.

By reading this document, the reader agrees that under no circumstances is the author responsible for any losses, direct or indirect, that are incurred as a result of the use of the information contained within this document, including, but not limited to, errors, omissions, or inaccuracies.

# CONTENTS

| | |
|---|---|
| *Introduction* | 7 |
| 1. THE UNFAIR ADVANTAGE | 13 |
| The Ones Who've Come Before | 15 |
| The 10 Benefits of Effective Communication | 20 |
| 2. WHERE IT ALL BEGINS | 29 |
| First Impressions Always Matter | 31 |
| Tips for Making a GREAT First Impression | 33 |
| Don'ts of First Impressions | 43 |
| Recovering From a Bad First Impression | 46 |
| 3. CONFIDENCE CHECK | 51 |
| Breathing | 53 |
| Self-Affirmation | 55 |
| Mindfulness | 61 |
| Cutting Negative Self-Talk | 68 |
| Preparation | 70 |
| Visualization | 73 |
| 4. MASTERING SMALL TALK | 77 |
| The Small Talk Mindset | 79 |
| Small Talk Topics | 82 |
| It's Not as Bad as It Sounds | 90 |
| From Small Talk to Big Talk | 93 |

5. BUILDING RELATIONSHIPS								99
The Importance of Healthy Work
Relationships									101
How to Build Good Relationships With
Colleagues									105
Influence vs. Manipulation							115

6. CONNECT AND CAPTIVATE WITH
STORIES									121
Storytelling as a Tool							124
The Four Types of Stories							127
How to Tell a Great Story							130
Getting People to Share Their Stories					134

7. TABOO TOPICS								137
Tips for Navigating Polarizing Topics					140
Expand Your Perspective of Others					144

8. THE CRAZIES								147
Dealing With Conflict							149
Dealing With Gossip							151
Dealing With Your Boss							155

*Conclusion*									159
*References*									165

## YOUR FREE GIFT!

As a thank you for purchasing my book, I would love to give you a free gift! This book is chock-full of everything you need to talk to anyone at work, but for all the recovering awkwards out there, it extends way beyond just work. Don't miss out on this list of the best resources for you along your journey to becoming *recovered* awkward person.

https://bit.ly/resources4awkwards

# INTRODUCTION

Have you ever met someone so confident and mature that it appears as if they are radiating success and interest, just to discover that they are your age, or worse, a couple of years younger than you are? Usually, what follows such an encounter is thinking to yourself how you'll never be as confident and successful as Karen, also known as Little Miss Perfect. Her smile never falters, yet everyone takes her seriously. She is friendly, yet the whole world seems to stop and listen when she speaks. She is kind yet strong. And even though she runs the show and demands to be taken seriously, she is still well-liked and seems to get along with everyone. Which begs the question: How the heck does she do it? How can she achieve all of the above, while you can barely greet the receptionist at the doctor's office

## 8 | INTRODUCTION

without feeling socially awkward and regretting every life decision you've ever made?

Well, she can achieve confidence, success, and well-liked because she uses a magic spell called "Good Communication." Yes, I know, it sounds cliche and overrated, but I can assure you it is anything but. Good communication can transform your entire world. It grants you self-confidence, it demands respect, it cultivates genuine relationships, and above all, it nips awkwardness in the butt!

It's hard to be confident in the workplace, especially as a woman. If you're too friendly, you might be considered the office pushover; but if you take things too seriously, all of a sudden, you're deemed the office witch. It's gotten to a point where many women avoid speaking to anyone at work because they're terrified of judgment and being considered socially awkward. Unfortunately, this often leads to a lack of professional advancement and being scared to speak out and step on someone's toes. Many women are also scared of destroying relationships if they're seen as too ambitious, so they refrain from talking about themselves and their successes.

Are you consumed with awkwardness, fear, and self-doubt? Do you feel stuck and disrespected in your career simply because you're scared of building relationships and unable to speak confidently to others? Do you crave self-confidence and success? Then I have good news for you: You're in the right place. Over the next eight chapters, we'll embark on a journey to discover the magical spell of communication that Little Miss Perfect possesses. The goal of this book is:

- To teach you the importance of good communication in the workplace and how it can lead to success.
- To show you how to make a good impression and never be seen as "that awkward lady" again.
- To equip you with the right tools and knowledge to remain confident in every situation, no matter how awkward or stressful.
- To help you become a master of small talk and how to transition into meaningful conversations.
- To encourage you to build meaningful relationships with authenticity.
- To equip you with storytelling tools to ensure that you captivate your audience and connect with others on a deeper level.
- To show you how to have those polarizing, taboo conversations about race, religion, etc., with ease.

## 10 | INTRODUCTION

- And lastly, we'll show you how to deal with
  THAT guy... You know the one-two offices
  down who speaks loudly and rudely and who
  makes you want to bang your head against the
  wall? Yeah, THAT guy! This book will tell you
  how to talk to even the most annoying, difficult
  people, making it possible to work with
  anyone!

If you're wondering who the heck I am to teach you all these things, I'm happy to report that I am no one special. I'm simply a recovered, awkward person who strives to succeed while being likable. For the longest time, I struggled to thrive in the workplace, terrified of upsetting others or embarrassing myself. So, I started investigating why I felt too awkward to just introduce myself, and I learned a great deal. I am incredibly passionate about this topic, and I know that if I didn't learn what I'm about to teach you, I would never have been able to pursue the career of my dreams: Podcast host. I went from being the shyest kid in the classroom to interviewing successful entrepreneurs worldwide while talking about serious topics. What I'm about to share with you in these eight chapters is what trans-formed me into someone who is confident and communicates clearly. Additionally, I've trained under some of the top minds in psychology, desperate to understand exactly why and how people communicate.

But above all of these things, I am simply someone who gets it.

I understand your awkward struggle and daily battle.

I understand your lack of self-confidence and constant fear.

I understand your social anxiety and know it's more than just "being a little shy."

I understand your struggle to achieve greatness while being held back by crippling fear.

I get it. I got through it. And so will you.

If you're ready to embark on this journey, join me, and together, we'll step out of awkwardness and into self-confidence that radiates success and likeability. Like Little Miss Perfect, you'll find yourself and your confidence in whom you are, equipped with the right communication skills to back it up. This is not a "quick fix" but rather a learning, applying, and assessing process. You won't wake up feeling 100% confident tomorrow, but perhaps you'll feel a little more encouraged to speak up. Together, we'll build your confidence and set you up for success.

12 | INTRODUCTION

Are you ready to embark on this life-changing journey? If the answer is yes, meet me in chapter one. If the answer is no, surprise yourself and do it anyway. Remember, you can't wait for confidence to find you; you must cultivate it situation by situation. I believe in you, and trust me, if I could shake my awkwardness, so can you!

1

# THE UNFAIR ADVANTAGE

I used to look at my colleagues who naturally communicated with others so effortlessly and be filled with jealousy. It felt like they had an unfair advantage in life and our professional careers. As a student, I saw the same thing when I was a server at a local restaurant. No matter how effectively I took up orders, delivered the food, and followed up on drink orders, I never received the same number of tips as some of my colleagues who constantly messed up. The most significant difference was: They chatted, smiled, and even made the customers laugh. They bonded and made the customers feel seen. I used to blame it on being an introvert, thinking everyone else had to be an extrovert. I hid behind being an introvert as if it was an excuse for being shy and awkward instead of working on ways to improve it. I claimed being awkward as my personality and it got me absolutely nowhere. I passed on fantastic opportunities and missed out on many life-changing moments simply because I felt "shy." One day, as I was working my shift at the restaurant, one of my fellow waiters turned to me and told me to chat more. Naturally, I told him I couldn't because I'm an introvert. He looked at me, laughed, and then shrugged his shoulders and said, "So what? So am I. Do you think extroverts are the only ones allowed to be successful?"

It made me think, and I realized that my answer was yes. I did think that only extroverts were allowed to be successful and able to communicate freely and boldly. I never even considered that communication was a skill anyone could learn, myself included. It was only years later that I acted on the truth and started investigating what communication is and how I could improve how I communicated. Communication takes various forms, and these days it's imperative to communicate not just as a person but as a brand. Luckily for us, there have been many successful entrepreneurs before us who have paved the way to communicating effectively for us. Let's look at some of the most successful entrepreneurs and how they used communication to achieve their success.

## THE ONES WHO'VE COME BEFORE

Most CEOs "believe that reputation is the single most important asset their company has" (Weverbergh & Vermoesen, 2022). How you present yourself will ultimately lead to your reputation, whether as a brand or as an individual. Rebranding yourself is very much like rebranding an organization. You are the CEO of your life, and it's your responsibility to take control of your reputation and how you present yourself. When you present yourself as the "too shy to speak up" employee, how can you expect your boss and colleagues to see you as anything else? The first step to battling your social anxiety and ever-looming awkwardness is recognizing the importance of communication and then communicating according to your brand. For example, if a brand claims to be family-oriented but uses swear words in its marketing material, would you believe them? Of course not! So, if you want to be considered a leader, innovator, and successful employee, you need to communicate accordingly and not hide away in your office or cubicle. It's all about building your personal brand, which we'll learn more about in Chapter five. For now, let's look at the experts and see how we can interpret it personally.

### Steve Jobs

Public Relations (PR) is a form of CEO communication. It's taking control of your image and how the public views you. Steve Jobs understood the urgency of PR from the beginning and onboarded Regis McKenna, one of the leading tech PR agents in Silicon Valley. PR is all about getting your image right the first time and giving the public what they want. They understood that the public loves a young entrepreneur, so naturally, Jobs became the face of his brand and handled all product launches, a practice many other organizations now use. Jobs also understood the power of communicating with brand users and started using his influence to auction exclusive interviews and meet with users face to face (Weverbergh & Vermoesen, 2022). As a result, Jobs is now known in the industry for his legendary launches! We can implement Jobs' CEO communication by being actively involved in building our public image and having a hands-on approach to communicating.

### Tony Hsieh

Tony Hsieh started as the CEO of Zappos, an online shoe retailer, but he realized he could sell something more significant than shoes: Happiness. Hsieh knew precisely how to make customers happy and even wrote a book about it. He communicated to the public, not just about the product itself but what it represents, happiness. He sold not just a product but a feeling. Eventually, he even created a tour bus called "Happiness," which travels around the US, accompanied by Tony himself and his vision (Weverbergh & Vermoesen, 2022). By communicating the feeling behind the product, he connected to his consumers and other thought leaders and generated a corporate culture geared towards making customers happy. We can learn from Tony and implement the idea of emotion into our way of communicating. The best way to connect with others is through emotions, which we'll discuss later.

### Rupert Murdoch

Rupert Murdoch, CEO of Myspace, became known for his transparency and authentic voice when he took to Twitter in an honest and raw way. Instead of relying on traditional media to tell his story, he decided to take to Twitter to be more transparent and open with consumers. Murdoch is now known for his transparency, authenticity, and admiring tone. By making himself available to the public, he shattered the image of a distant CEO, replacing it with an online presence accessible to all (Weverbergh & Vermoesen, 2022). We can learn a lot from Murdoch. Not only was it unconventional of him to join Twitter at such an old stage, but he created his personal brand by being transparent and authentic, something all of us should strive to be.

### Brené Brown

Research professor and master storyteller Brené Brown went viral for her TED talk in 2012. As the author of five bestselling books and a Netflix special called The Call to Courage, Brown knows her story and has been deemed a phenomenal leader. Her secret? Vulnerability. According to Brown, "vulnerability is our most accurate measurement of courage" (Slack, 2019). Brown finds confidence in vulnerability, something that most people shy away from.

What is more vulnerable than creating something out of nothing and showing it to the world? Being yourself takes courage and requires a lot of vulnerability. Vulnerability is the key to opening up to colleagues. We can learn from Brown to seek courage and not comfort and to see being vulnerable as being brave instead of awkward.

### Scott Kelly

Scott Kelly is an American astronaut known for his incredible bravery and leadership skills (Slack, 2019). Despite the tension between the United States and Russia, Kelly worked with Russian cosmonaut Mikhail Kornieko to display unity and solidarity. Although politics often gets in the way of the mission, Kelly and Kornieko rose above it and found common ground. They worked together and achieved great things as a space duo. Being friends with the people you work with is not a requirement, but if there is something you both believe in, it will have mutual benefits. It takes a great leader to recognize the importance of common ground, and we can take this page from Kelly's book and add it to our own. Instead of being afraid of collaboration, we should seek common ground to remove awkwardness.

### Michelle Obama

Michelle Obama is known for her perfect composure, mixed with candor and humor. The former First Lady speaks frankly about her marriage, role as a mom, and responsibility as a woman. She also shares openly about her struggle with social anxiety and her fears of not being respected as an individual in her own right. Obama is known for connecting with audiences through humor and authenticity instead of a persona of perfection. She believes that one of the smartest things you can do as a leader is to allow those around you to be authentic (Slack, 2019). She also believes that your personal life is a story you own and something that no one can take away from you; therefore, you should own it. We should take this advice into our daily lives. Instead of feeling awkward when we do something that is simply just "us," own it. We will dive deeper into owning it and vulnerability in chapter five.

When we look at these leaders and how they approach life, we can see that they have similar values: authenticity, transparency, and collaboration. Of course, effective communication can lead to these values being visible in our lives as well, but these aren't the only benefits of effective communication. So let's take a closer look at some other benefits of effective communication.

## THE 10 BENEFITS OF EFFECTIVE COMMUNICATION

As I mentioned earlier, there are different types of communication. To be considered an effective communicator, you need to be able to communicate clearly in all four areas: verbal, nonverbal, visual, and written. You will enjoy the benefits when you can communicate effectively in all areas.

### 1. Builds Trust

Effective communication cultivates trust between you and others. Listening attentively and embracing different views will show others that you can be trusted, whether in your personal or work life. It is a two-way street, so to be trusted, you must also learn how to trust. When you trust others and show your team that you can be trusted, you can fulfill your duties better (CLIMB, 2019). Think about it, who do you trust most in your life? Is it that guy at work who never really gives you a straight answer, or is it the colleague who speaks clearly, gives you regular updates, and always involves you in the process? Exactly! Therefore, you need to be the one who communicates clearly in order to be trusted by others.

## 2. Resolves Conflict

Conflict in the workplace is inevitable. You spend so much time with your colleagues that it's almost impossible to never run into hiccups. I know conflict is a terrifying thought, but conflict can be resolved painlessly with effective communication. Part of effective communication is remaining calm, listening to everyone, and finding an ideal solution for everyone involved (CLIMB, 2019). When you can do that, conflict can actually be a good thing! Not only does good communication resolve conflict quickly, but it also prevents conflict. When everyone is open, vulnerable, and honest, there will be less space for miscommunication and conflict (Indeed Editorial Team, 2021).

### 3. Provides Clarity and Direction

With good communication comes clear goal-setting and expectations. A lot of confusion in the workplace results from uncommunicated expectations. When you have a certain expectation of a colleague or team member, voice it kindly, so they understand what you want from them. When they know what you expect from them, they'll be able to work towards a clear goal with direction (CLIMB, 2019). Effective communication will also give you a sense of peace, knowing that those around you know what to expect from you, eliminating confusion and anxiety.

### 4. Creates Stronger Relationships

You will create stronger relationships with others when you communicate clearly, listen attentively, and provide quality feedback. All most people want in this world is to be listened to and feel seen. With effective communication, you can do this while maintaining healthy work boundaries. Showing your colleagues that you listen to them and are invested in their work will cultivate mutual respect and build a stronger relationship (CLIMB, 2019). If you work with clients, effective communication will lead to better relationships with them too. How you talk and listen to your clients goes a long way. Most clients prefer working with agencies and organizations that care about them rather than the one with the cheapest offer (Indeed Editorial Team, 2021). Furthermore, leaders who cultivate strong relationships with their team through effective communication see less turnover and stronger devotion from their employees, which leads to the next benefit.

### 5. Increases Engagement

The most successful organizations have employees who are engaged in the process and the mission of the brand. The more confident you feel in your work, the more engaged you'll be. According to a recent study, only 15% of adult employees are engaged with their work and employers (CLIMB, 2019). When you prioritize effective communication, you invite other employees to buy into their work and be invested as team members. Clear communication helps management to understand the goals and the needs of the employees, so be sure to communicate your specific needs and wants to your employer. The better the communication, the more engaged you'll be in your career.

### 6. Improves Productivity

Have you ever felt like you were just a cog in a big machine that keeps marching forward? No matter how terrible the system is, and no matter what you say or do, it keeps trudging you forward. In a situation like that, it's almost impossible to try and be productive because what's the point anyway. However, when you feel heard and understood by your employer, you will most likely be more committed and productive. Good communication leads to better productivity, especially when working in a team. When you have a team project, be sure to communicate each team member's role and responsibility. Having clear marching orders will help overall productivity, and it can illuminate whether one member is bulldozing over the others and doing everything themselves (Indeed Editorial Team, 2021). Clear communication also leads to better organization, and better organization leads to improved productivity.

### 7. Promotes Team Building

The more effective the communication in a team, the more members will be able to rely on each other. When you work together as a team and reach your goals, it creates a sense of camaraderie. The better you work in a team, the more likely others will want to work with you (CLIMB, 2019). If your contribution to the team is keeping quiet and not voicing your feedback, chances are that others won't see you as invested and might not want to work with you again. If you practice effective communication, you might find that teamwork is actually fun and beneficial. The more you work with certain colleagues, the closer your relationship will be, and the more you'll be able to work together seamlessly.

## 8. Creates Healthy Culture

You might be expected to work with people from different backgrounds and cultures in the workplace. A healthy work environment creates a safe space for all cultures to feel at home. Unfortunately, with "cancel culture," we've become scared of speaking to other cultures, afraid we might offend. Cancel culture is a phrase used to refer to when someone is being called out for something they did, either online or in person. When you "cancel" someone, you aim to destroy their image, career, and personal life. Cancel culture took off in the last couple of years, and it appears that everyone is looking for reasons to cancel others. Because of Cancel Culture, everyone seems to be walking on eggshells, terrified of offending someone and being called out for it.

In order to create a healthy environment, you have to be able to communicate with people from different cultures the same way you would someone from your own culture. The best way to do this is to speak openly with your colleagues and ask them whether something is appropriate. Instead of avoiding them, open an honest conversation where both parties can learn from one another. With open communication, you can prevent mishaps and create an open culture where everyone is welcome. It's not about being perfect and never making mistakes but about having meaningful conversations. Open communication fosters an accepting environment where everyone feels equal (Indeed Editorial Team, 2021).

### 9. Increases Innovations

Where there is open communication, more ideas will flow, and more innovation will be cultivated. Just think about it: When do you feel most creative? In an environment where you are scared to speak, or one where all ideas are welcome, no matter how big or small? Chances are that you'll feel more comfortable in an environment that welcomes ideas than in an environment where no one speaks openly. In addition, when open communication is encouraged in the workplace, employees feel more empowered to think differently (Indeed Editorial Team, 2021). Effective communication welcomes different ideas and thoughts and encourages employees to bounce ideas off one another.

### 10. Boosts Satisfaction

When you are part of an organization that practices good communication, you are more likely to experience job satisfaction (Indeed Editorial Team, 2021). The same goes for one-on-one conversations. You'll be more satisfied with the overall encounter when you walk out of a conversation feeling understood, heard, and acknowledged. A transparent environment encourages open communication, leading to an enjoyable outcome for all parties involved. The more effective the communication, the less frustrating it will be for employees.

As you can see, effective communication is highly beneficial in both the workplace and your personal life. The International Journal of Management and Business Studies went so far as to say that good communication doesn't only help a team to complete their project. However, it enables an organization to succeed and grow (Slack, 2019). In your personal life, it works the same. With good communication, you can succeed and grow no matter what you face. Just like all the leaders we looked at in this chapter, you can achieve greatness through your way of communicating. As we continue this journey, you'll find that what appeared to be an unfair advantage for others (like Little Miss Perfect) will be your greatest weapon and tool for success. In the next chapter, we'll look at where good communication starts: a solid first impression.

2

## WHERE IT ALL BEGINS

Have you ever met someone and immediately thought, "Uhm, no." You know what I'm talking about, right? Maybe it was a colleague or friend of a friend that you simply just don't like and don't really have a good reason why. It's just a feeling... Well, sorry to burst your bubble. It's probably not just a feeling. It's probably because of a bad first impression. Let me explain.

One of my closest friends, Jason, met the girl of his dreams a couple of years ago. For the first time ever, he was excited about settling down, meeting the family, and building a life together. So, after a couple of weeks, he got invited to her parent's house for a dinner party. He really wanted to make a good impression, so he stopped at the store to pick up a fancy bottle of wine and flowers on his way there. As he left the store, the bottle of wine fell and spilled all over his clothes. Already a couple of minutes late and with no time to turn around and change outfits, he got into the car and started driving. He carefully held the flowers in his lap, which caused a massive allergy attack. How was he supposed to know he was allergic to roses and chivalry? He was about five minutes away when a traffic officer pulled him over. With the wine all over him and red eyes from the flowers, it took some serious convincing and a breathalyzer test for the officer not to arrest him for drunk driving. When he finally arrived at the dinner party, it wasn't a good look.

For almost an entire year, her family was convinced that he was a drunken frat boy who was always late and drunk. Then, finally, they got to know the real Jason and, what do you know, they actually liked him. If only he had made a better first impression, things might have been much easier on them the first few months of dating.

You see, how you present yourself the first time influences everything that comes after that. Making a good first impression is extremely important if you want to ace the test of social interaction and success, but it's not as easy as it sounds. Making a good first impression depends on how you look (spilled wine, isn't it), how you hold yourself, and the very first thing that comes out of your mouth. In retrospect, Jason probably shouldn't have entered the house with the words, "I almost got arrested just now!"

This chapter will discuss the importance of an excellent first impression, tips for making a great first impression, and how you can recover from a bad first impression (yes, it's possible). So, get ready. It's time to put your best foot forward!


## FIRST IMPRESSIONS ALWAYS MATTER

There are a few things that last a lifetime: A Twinkie, a cockroach, and a first impression. Whether accurate or not, first impressions have a way of sticking around. It is something you will never forget. Perhaps you have a friend whom you didn't like at first. Chances are you still talk and laugh about your "first impression" of each other. Just think about your life real quick. What was your first impression of the person you love the most? And what about the person you despise? Chances are that you probably have a pretty clear memory of that encounter. Why? Because first impressions are primarily subconscious. Due to cognitive biases, we see the world and people through our own set of lenses and filters that we use to judge others (Waters, 2021). Therefore, every encounter you have will be affected by the first impression that you make. Whether it's a good or a bad one isn't always in your control, but there are a few things that you can do to increase the chances of an excellent first impression.

So, take a moment and ask yourself: What first impression would I like to make?

If people's first impression of you is that you are bubbly, friendly, and competent, they will most likely feel more comfortable around you than someone who appears closed-off, mysterious, and angsty. Regarding career life, making an excellent first impression can make the world's difference. It might get you a job or a future opportunity. Alternatively, it might help you network and be recommended by other professionals (Waters, 2021). Making a good first impression can help you to achieve success and reach your goals while making a bad first impression might add some obstacles to your journey.

To confirm just how important first impressions are, a study was conducted at Longwood University. First, researchers asked students to evaluate their professors after meeting them. They then asked the same students to assess the same professors after the semester, and the results showed that the evaluations didn't differ (Buchert et al., 2008). Furthermore, the first impressions that the students had of the professors remained the same throughout the entire semester, proving just how strong first impressions can be and how important it is to make a good one.

That being said, let's look at how you can make not just a good first impression but a great one that will boost you closer to success.

## TIPS FOR MAKING A GREAT FIRST IMPRESSION

As mentioned earlier, a good impression depends on how you look, how you carry yourself, and what you say. Verbal and nonverbal communication is critical when making a first impression, and you should be aware of what you are communicating with your body. So, let's start with the first part of making a GREAT impression: How you look.

### How You Look

According to researchers, it takes a mere seven seconds to make a first impression (Psychology Today, 2011). I want you to quickly imagine yourself sitting in a restaurant, about to meet someone new. As you sit by the window, you see a taxi pull up. You watch as the passenger gets out, smiles at the taxi driver, and gives him a generous tip. You watch as the person walks up to the restaurant door, holding it open for the mom-

and-stroller, who is struggling to manage with only two hands. You notice smiles as kind greetings are exchanged. You do a once-over and notice their well-polished shoes and ironed shirt. They spot you, smile, and as they make their way over to you, seven seconds have passed, and you already know that you'll like them.

In many cases, the first seven seconds of a first impression will be completely silent, as in the scenario above. So you'll have to rely on nonverbal communication to make an excellent first impression within seven seconds. Sounds challenging? Well, it's actually easier than you might think; you just need to be aware of a couple of things.

## What is Your Body Language Saying

If the person you were meeting in the restaurant did everything exactly the way they just did, but instead of kindly helping the mom at the door, they annoyingly tapped their foot, would you still feel the same way about them? Probably not, no. That's because your body language is a massive part of communication, and when your body language isn't positive, it will influence your first impression negatively (Waters, 2021). This is because your body and emotions are connected, which is referred to as "The Feedback Loop." The feedback loop signifies that whatever your body is communicating is the emotion you will experience, and whatever emotion you experience, that is the message your body will convey. For example, if your body language is screaming, "I am anxious!" you will experience anxiety within you. By calming your body language, you also calm your inner emotions and thoughts. Let's take a look at a few examples:

- If you tap your foot while waiting for someone or something, you're communicating to your emotions that you are frustrated and annoyed, which will immediately be displayed on your face.
- By crossing your arms in conversation, you communicate to yourself and others that you are closed off and not easily impressed.
- If you shake someone's hand so firmly that they need to see a surgeon afterward, you're communicating that you're full of yourself and highly competitive.

Take a moment to reflect on your own body language. What do you think your body is communicating to your mind and to others? Are you slouching, showing that you're insecure? Or do you have good posture, not scared of enjoying your time in the sun? Compare your findings with what you said you wanted your first impression to be. Do they align? If not, take some time to address your body language and identify areas where you can improve.

**Say It With Your Face**

The following way in which you can improve your nonverbal first impression is to say it with your face. Making eye contact is extremely important when meeting someone for the first time. I know it feels awkward at first, especially if you're socially awkward in general, but making eye contact can be a reason why people may find you trustworthy or not. Eye contact shows respect, and it is taken as a show of honesty (Waters, 2021). So, when someone is talking to you, keep eye contact. When your eyes wander, you're communicating to the other person that you're not interested in what they're saying and that they don't deserve your undivided attention. Be warned, though; there is a difference between making eye contact and staring someone down. Try to keep eye contact for 60% of the interaction. If you stare someone down, it might appear as if you are distrusting of them or being aggressive.

Another way that you can say it with your face is by smiling. Yes, I know, the general response to "You should smile more" is immediate frowning and distaste, but a sincere smile can go a long way. No, I'm not saying that you should turn into an actor in a toothpaste commercial. Instead, put people at ease with a comfortable, genuine smile. A smile should always reach your eyes; otherwise, you might look like a lifeless doll who hates their life. In addition, a genuine smile creates the impression of trust and sincerity (Waters, 2021).

I have a friend with the most amazing smile! When you read novels, and they describe a character with a smile that can "light up even the darkest room," that's the kind of smile this friend of mine has. She can convey so much emotion and understanding in her smile that it not only lights up the room but also validates you simultaneously. That's because not only does she have a fantastic smile, but she is a master of all facial expressions. She listens actively and shows you that she is listening by expressing every emotion you hope to see when you tell your story. She displays how you're feeling or how shocking the story is that you're describing. She uses not only her mouth to smile, but her eyes, cheeks, and forehead all work together to create these intense expressions. It makes you feel comfortable, understood, and heard. That is the power of a great smile! So, my friend, don't hold back when you're smiling. Let your emotions run wild and shine through your entire face! It isn't just beneficial for you, but it allows others to open up and trust you, and it enables long-term relationship building without you doing any of the talking.

## Dress to Impress

The final way to ensure an excellent first impression during those first seven seconds of nonverbal communication is by making sure that you're dressed to impress. Like Roxette said in 1988, you're "gonna get dressed for success" if you want to make it big. What you wear says a lot about who you are. Now, am I saying that you should get out the stockings and court shoes when going to the grocery store? Of course not! But maybe change the shirt with ketchup stains for one that is comfortable and casual yet says, "I take care of myself and shower regularly." Again, what you wear contributes significantly to your first impression (Waters, 2021). Even when people claim not to be phased by what others are wearing, subconsciously, everyone judges each other based on their appearance. So be sure to dress appropriately for the occasion, which means being careful of overdressing. When you dress too casually, you might give the impression that you aren't serious about the situation (Waters, 2021). If you're ever in doubt, err on the side of caution and dress up a little.

### How You Carry Yourself

You can be the best-dressed person in the room, but you will fade into the shadows if you lack confidence. So even when you don't feel brave, do it scared. Put on your brave face, correct your posture, and be true to who you are. Making a good first impression is not about pretending to be someone else but simply about presenting the best version of yourself. Two things are essential in how you carry yourself: Authenticity and confidence.

### Be Authentic

Regardless of what we think, most people subconsciously can immediately pick up whether someone is authentic or simply pretending to be someone else. When you're authentic to who you are, you invite others to do the same. It's much easier to trust someone who is authentic because what you see is what you get. Despite what people might claim to want, no one really wants a "yes-man." You know, that one colleague who just agrees with everything you do and says yes to everything you ask even when you know they don't agree? That's a "yes-man." They'll agree with anything to your face, despite what they'll later say to others. Being authentic eliminates all "yes-man" actions and shows others that you can be trusted.

**Confidence Is Key**

To make an excellent first impression, you must carry yourself confidently. Pulling at your clothes, looking down, and twiddling your thumbs are all signs that you lack confidence. Be careful, though; there is a fine line between being confident and cocky. You don't want to be like Brad, who thinks he can do no wrong and claims to always have the answers. Be confident in who you are, and then be who you are. Being confident can look different for every personality, but some things just scream confidence, like:

- Eye contact
- Smiling
- Good posture
- Speaking up for yourself
- Resting your hands on the table
- Not looking at your phone

*What You Say*

The final thing that determines the quality of your first impression depends on what you say. Your first sentence is crucial, whether you're personally meeting someone for the first time or going for a job interview. People will forever connect your first words to who they think you are, which means that if you don't say anything, they'll probably assume you're too shy to handle big clients or make a case for the company. You can ensure you say the right thing by following these three guidelines.

## Listen

After you've greeted the other person, be sure to listen to what they are saying. Have you ever had a conversation similar to this one:

You: Hi, it's nice to meet you.
Person: Hi, how are you?
You: Good, thanks, and you?
Person: Okay, and you?
*awkward stares and nods*

Sounds familiar? That's because the person you're talking to is just going through the motions and not really listening to your response. So to make a good first impression, listen carefully to what the other person is saying and respond accordingly.

## Be Prepared

If you're going to a work function and meeting other professionals, do your homework. If you know another company that might be there that you don't know much about, do a quick google search in preparation.

Let's say the company has a new product launching soon and has been advertising on social media; you can ask them how their campaign is coming along. Or if some big news just came out in their industry that they have been commenting about, read a few of their posts or dive into their blog to use as a conversation starter. You can also ask them how they're dealing with the new industry changes or whether they've recovered fully after the pandemic. Having something to talk about will help to remove the awkwardness and smooth out the beginnings of conversations seamlessly. If you're going for an interview or meeting a new client, do proper research on the organization. Being prepared will put you at ease, making you more comfortable and showing the other party that you care enough to be prepared. Being prepared for a meeting is a way of showing respect.

**Respect**

Whatever you say, say it with respect. No matter if you know the person or not, agree with their statement or not, and have respect for all other human beings. A lack of respect is the quickest way of signing away your good first impression forever. In all conversations, be aware of the cultures involved and represented communities. I'm not saying to avoid all difficult or controversial conversations, quite the opposite, really, but be sure to approach these conversations with the utmost respect, as if talking to your hero. Remember, you can't get anywhere in a conversation if you don't first and foremost respect their opinion and point of view. Always approach a conversation with an open mind and as a chance to discover something new. Even if all you are learning is the incredulous way that the person thinks.

## DON'TS OF FIRST IMPRESSIONS

Now that we know what we should do to make a good first impression, there are also a few big red flags you should avoid, like the plague. In my book, there are four don'ts of a first impression that you should never entertain, and (although I'm not proud to say!) I can honestly admit that I have done all four of these things in the past. So let's have a look.

### Oversharing Is Not Caring

Yes, authenticity is key, and part of being authentic is sharing who you are and some life stories, but there is such a thing as OVERsharing. Perhaps your possible new employer doesn't need to know that you struggle with Irritable Bowel Syndrome and that Jazz music is your favorite workout music. It would be best to find a balance between being open and sharing and avoiding oversharing. Oversharing might put people off, and you don't want to be remembered as the jazzy-bowel woman forever, do you?

### Never Interrupt When Others Are Talki...

There are few things as disrespectful as interrupting someone while they talk. Although not always done out of malice or a lack of interest, interrupting someone shows them that you think you know better or simply don't care. A very good friend of mine was diagnosed with ADHD when he was a teenager. Frequently when people tell stories, he would get so excited that he started talking over them. For example, I would tell a story about fishing, which would remind him of that one time he went fishing as a kid, and he would feel the urgent need to tell the story immediately. Although he didn't mean it out of disrespect or disinterest, it still bothered me and others close to him. So, he started actively working on it. Although it is because of his ADHD and not because he wants to be rude, it was still in his control to manage his actions. Now, when he starts interrupting others, he takes a deep breath, apologizes, and then continues to listen.

### No Phone Zone

Have you ever tried telling someone a story, but they're constantly on their phone? No matter how hard you try, it feels impossible to enthusiastically continue the conversation when you know the other person isn't paying attention. If you want to make an excellent first impression, put your phone away and fight the urge to look at it during the conversation. For many of us, checking our phones has become a safe little bubble to avoid awkward eye contact, but it's time to put the phone away and look up. That includes not looking at your smartwatch every time it beeps with a notification. Instead, give the person your full attention. You'll have more than enough time to check your phone later.

### Are You Trying Too Hard?

I'm a big fan of the 1994 sitcom series Friends. In one of the later seasons, Phoebe meets her boyfriend's fancy parents for the first time. So, she asks Rachel to help her get dressed in something fancy and puts on an accent to sound more posh. But, of course, Phoebe being Phoebe, she gets nervous and overshares all of her darkest and weirdest stories. Instead of making a good first impression, she does everything wrong, no matter how hard she tries. Why? She was simply trying too hard. Of course, there's no way of knowing whether the parents would have liked her if she was just being herself, but it would have been much less painful to watch! Phoebe is usually very confident in her own skin, and it was almost sad to see her trying to be someone else.

When you try too hard to impress someone else, it's pretty obvious and often leads to the opposite happening, but don't worry; it's all salvageable.

## RECOVERING FROM A BAD FIRST IMPRESSION

As someone who is a little socially awkward and nervous about talking to people, you've probably made a few bad first impressions in your life. But don't worry, so have I and most other people, regardless of whether they are socially awkward or not. So, let's ask the important questions.

Is it possible to recover from a bad first impression? Yes.

Will it be easy? Probably not.

To overcome a bad first impression requires consistent effort and, ultimately, a little bit of time and patience. So let's look at a couple of things you can do to overcome a bad first impression.

### Accept It

The first step to overcoming a bad first impression is accepting that you've made a bad first impression. Once you've accepted that it didn't go well, ask yourself, "What is it that went wrong?" By identifying what went wrong, you become self-aware of what you need to improve on and change in the future to avoid making the same mistakes again. Maybe what went wrong is that you tried too hard, so next time, relax and be yourself. Perhaps you didn't speak at all, so next time, tell a personal story that is funny and engaging. When you know what went wrong, it's easier to take corrective action.

### Admit and Apologize

After you've accepted that it didn't go well and discovered what went wrong, ask yourself whether you did something wrong. Perhaps you said something offensive or showed a lack of interest by being on your phone to avoid eye contact. Whatever the case, admit that you did something wrong. Then, ask yourself whether it requires an apology. If you did something slightly awkward or didn't talk at all, it might be better just to correct your action since an apology might make things even more awkward. However, step up and apologize if you said something offensive or showed up late all soaked in wine (Like Jason did). By apologizing, you'll let the other person know you are aware of the issue and want to improve. By apologizing, you show that you are invested in the person's first impression of you (Waters, 2021).

### Look to the Future

Don't obsess about the failed first impression. When you dwell on the past, it will make moving on very hard. Instead, focus on your actions in the future; rather than lying awake replaying the awkward first impression, brainstorm ways to improve it. Overthinking will probably make you feel even more awkward, which is something we should definitely try to avoid. Try to avoid the death trap of "If only I didn't" and instead focus on what you can do next time instead. Make a few mental notes like "don't look at your phone" or "remember to smile" instead of beating yourself up about something small.

### Be Consistent

The final step in correcting a bad first impression is to be consistent in who you are going forward. Just like my friend Jason who had to wait a while and show up on time for all the other occasions, you'll have to show them who you really are until the first impression is just a distant memory. Your consistency will ultimately show your sincerity (Waters, 2021). Any lapse in your positive actions will only reinforce their first bad impression of you. If Jason were to show up late to the second and the third dinner party or post photos of him drinking on social media, it would show the family that they were right in their first impression of him as a drunken frat boy. Instead, he showed up early, dressed nicely and neatly, and made sure never to mention getting almost arrested again.

To summarize, a good first impression can open a lot of positive doors for you, filled with work and personal opportunities. Take some time and assess your first impression with others. Ask your close friends and trusted colleagues for their first impression of you. There might be something small that you are doing that is offensive or coming across as ignorant or uninterested. Be open to change and open to admit that there is something you can do about it. The days of blaming it on your personality type are over. Of course, sometimes life happens, and you do something embarrassing, but that's okay. In the next chapter, we'll discuss maintaining confidence no matter what happens.

# 3

## CONFIDENCE CHECK

I remember the first time I had to present something at work. Like a bad nightmare, it haunts me to this very day. My stomach was rumbling louder than a monster truck, flipping and turning with every thought. My throat was a desert while simultaneously forming copious amounts of saliva, while my tongue felt numb. My brain suddenly couldn't "English," and my hands were shaking enough to cool down the entire boardroom. I got through it with a couple of "uhms," but it was survivable. As I came to the end, I exhaled a deep breath of relief, ready to take my seat, when the unthinkable happened…

Questions. My boss and colleagues had questions.

In my preparation for the presentation, I never even considered questions. I knew the answers; that wasn't my problem. I just didn't know how to tell them that I knew the answers without fainting or worse, saying something awkward! My cheeks flushed red, my breathing became rapid, and from the corner of my eye, I saw someone mouth, "Shame, this poor dude." I was mortified. As I grabbed the glass of water in front of me, desperately looking for a way to clean out the desert in my throat, I spilled half of the glass all over my shirt. As I apologized, I realized that I didn't bring water to the meeting and that I had just drowned myself in my boss's water.

I was certain that my life, and my career, were over. Completely ready to crawl into a tiny space and die, my boss stood up, thanked me for all the work and research that I'd done, and made a joke about the water. He even told me that I did a great job and that he wouldn't have been able to do any better (a lie, but a comforting one). I was surprised at his calmness and awestruck by his confidence. As he was about to leave the boardroom, he looked at me and said, "Always stay confident. No matter how naked you feel."

Have you ever experienced awkwardness on such a level that it feels impossible to remain confident? Well, the truth is that with the right tools and exercises, anyone can remain confident, no matter the severity of the situation. If you want to be able to talk to anyone, you need to learn how to remain confident in yourself and in the way you carry yourself. Here's a tip I wish I had known sooner: It's only awkward if you allow it to be. If you own who you are and the mistakes you make, no one else will feel awkward or whisper "this poor girl" behind gritted teeth.

In this chapter, we'll look at different techniques and practices that you can implement to always remain confident. From how you breathe to how you prepare, we'll cover it all and ensure confidence!

BREATHING

Breathing techniques have been part of meditation and mindfulness for many years, but many people don't know that breathing can be a powerful confidence booster when done correctly. When you're nervous, your breathing becomes shallow, your heart starts to race, and your mind gets flooded with "fight or flight" responses. So you remember in the previous chapter where we talked about the feedback loop? Well, it's the same with breathing. If your breathing spins out of control, you will be more anxious, and the more anxious you are, the more out of control your breathing will be. Somewhere we need to throw a spanner in the works and stop the loop from continuing. So, let me introduce you to "Breathing Exercises," our savior from the endless feedback loop.

Before we get into the specifics of breathing to calm ourselves down and remain confident, it's essential to know that there are different types of breathing. When you breathe just to live, it's called vegetative breathing, while breathing for speech is called active or controlled breathing (Genard, 2019). When you breathe for speech instead of just to live, you will feel more confident and find it easier to speak up and articulate clearly. So when you feel your breathing quickening because of fear, take a moment and tell yourself the following:

"Public speaking isn't dangerous."

You're not in a car chase or being stalked by a lion. You will be okay. It's just talking. When you tell yourself that it's not dangerous, your mind will respond by limiting the fight or flight responses, which will help your breathing to calm down physically (Genard, 2019). So, how do we breathe if we want to remain calm and confident? It's something called Diaphragmatic Breathing.

### Diaphragmatic Breathing

Funnily enough, diaphragmatic breathing has less to do with how you inhale and focuses more on exhalation.

When you inhale, your heart speeds up, and when you exhale, your heart slows down. So, when you focus more on exhaling, you focus on slowing you're your body, helping you remain calm. When you exhale for a more extended period of time, you go from "fight or flight" to "rest and digest" (Genard, 2019). Here's how you do it:

1. Breathe in for 4 seconds.
2. Hold your breath for another 4 seconds.
3. Exhale slowly for six seconds.
4. Pause for 2 seconds before repeating.

This is a gentle and easy way to communicate to your body that it can relax and be calm. So, next time you feel stressed, hide in the bathroom for a couple of minutes and practice this breathing style. Chances are you'll feel relaxed and more confident within just a few cycles.

SELF-AFFIRMATION

I want you to take a couple of minutes and think about the thoughts you have about yourself each day. How would the piles look if you had to label each thought as either positive or negative (Boynton, 2021)? Is your negative pile so high that it's about to fall over? How about your positive pile? Most of us have constant thoughts running through our minds, with an inner critic as the narrator. We constantly think and say things to ourselves that are mean, critical, and rude. Not sure what I'm talking about? Look at the list below and tell me whether these thoughts ever cross your mind.

- Why am I like this?
- I'll never get that promotion!
- I'm too awkward to talk to that person.
- Socializing with others? I'd rather stick needles in my eyes.
- This confrontation is going to be so awkward!
- If only you were prettier, you wouldn't be this awkward.
- Confidence is for people who deserve it. I'm just not built to be confident.
- I'm socially awkward, and that's how I'll always be.
- Of course, I won't be successful. Just look at me!
- I can be so stupid sometimes.
- I wish I could just hide away from everyone.

Having negative self-talk is not rare. Most people struggle with it, but it's in your control to do something about it. You'll never feel confident in your skin when you talk to yourself negatively. If you don't even like yourself and believe in yourself, how should others? Thoughts we think regularly change our brain's structure and make it easier to repeat the same negative thoughts repeatedly (Boynton, 2021). Basically, the more you tell yourself that you're awkward and lack confidence, the more awkward and lacking in confidence you'll be. So, how do we correct the inner critic and stop ourselves from making everything more awkward than it really is? The answer lies in positive self-affirmations.

Positive self-affirmations are a form of self-talk where you take conscious steps to better your view of yourself (Boynton, 2021). Traditionally, self-affirmations were short phrases you repeat to yourself throughout the day, but they have evolved since then. Positive self-affirmations don't have to be one phrase you repeat but rather finding ways to affirm yourself during the day. For example, if you interact with the guy at the coffee cart, give yourself a little pat on the back. If you managed to make eye contact with the receptionist, celebrate it! Use the small moments in the day to celebrate your progress and simply the fact that you are an awesome person. According to James Clear, author of Atomic Habits, you need to provide your brain with examples that prove you are the type of person you aspire to be (Attia, 2022).

If you want to set some positive self-affirmations, there are a few things that you should keep in mind. Let's quickly look at how to create the perfect positive self-affirmation.

### Meaningful

A self-affirmation must be meaningful to you. It doesn't have to make sense to anyone else as long as it's meaningful to you. If you want to call yourself a "beautiful peanut," and it truly makes your heart happy, then do it. The key is to make it as personal as possible; otherwise, it won't have the same effect. Think about what it is that you want to be and what role you want to have. Then, use that as motivation to create self-affirmation. For example, if you want to be the manager at your organization, whenever you do something good, say to yourself, "Now that's manager material." It might sound silly to others, but you're affirming yourself into the role you want, making you more confident once the opportunity presents itself.

### Practice

Once you've created your self-affirmation, you need to practice it. It might feel strange at first and a little awkward to compliment yourself instead of tearing yourself down, but the more you practice, the more natural it will become. Again, consistency is key; the more you affirm yourself, the less silly and awkward you'll feel. Once you get over the initial weirdness, you might even start to believe in yourself and act more confidently, which is the goal, after all. Breaking out of all patterns will also take some time, so whenever you catch yourself having a negative thought, replace it with a positive one and decide to focus on the good instead of the bad. Let's look at those negative self-talk examples we had earlier and see how we can turn them into something positive.

| Instead of... | Try... |
|---|---|
| Why am I like this? | What can I do differently next time, so I don't act that way again? |
| I'll never get that promotion! | What can I learn from Jen, who was the last one to get a promotion, so that I can be the next one on the list? |
| I'm too awkward to talk to that person. | How can I make myself feel confident before entering this conversation? |
| Socializing with others? I'd rather stick needles in my eyes. | I know I would rather do anything other than socialize right now, but is there something I can do to make this an enjoyable evening? |
| This confrontation is going to be so awkward! | Confrontation is part of life; it is good to talk about things that bother you. This will improve the relationship in the long run. |
| If only you were prettier, you wouldn't be this awkward. | I am enough just as I am. I can make a success of this conversation. I don't have to hide myself away. |
| Confidence is for people who deserve it. I'm just not built to be confident. | I deserve to be confident. I am fearless. I can talk to anyone I want to. I have achieved so much in my life already. |
| I'm socially awkward, and that's how I'll always be. | I don't have to feel this awkward forever. I can change my behavior and reactions and learn to be more confident in my skin. |
| Of course, I won't be successful. Just look at me! | I have everything I need to make a success out of my life and my career. Nothing is holding me back. |
| I can be so stupid sometimes. | I make mistakes, and that is okay. I'm just a human and can use my mistakes to learn and improve. |
| I wish I could just hide away from everyone. | Although I don't want to interact with people right now, I can hold a conversation and use this as a learning experience. |

## *Delete the Critic*

If you want self-affirmation to work, you must eliminate your inner critic. We'll talk more about this in the section about cutting negative self-talk, but for now, it's important to recognize your inner critic. When you recognize you are being mean to yourself, you'll become more aware of the areas in which you need to be nicer to yourself (Boynton, 2021). For example, when your inner critic tries to tell you that you are not worthy of success or that you'll always be the shy, awkward girl who didn't have friends in the first grade, tell it to be quiet and affirm yourself with everything you've accomplished in your life.

For example, if your inner critic tells you that the presentation will fail because you're not a good public speaker, take a moment to correct the thought. Remember the times when you were a success and when you spoke publicly without issues. Gather evidence from your past experiences as proof that the critic is wrong, and then use self-affirmations to keep your confidence levels high.

## MINDFULNESS

We all have an autopilot mode that we rely on when things are busy, a little crazy, or completely out of control. Our autopilot mode is how we naturally deal with chaos or things not going according to plan (which they rarely do). It's how you cope with trauma and tragedy, manage stress and conflict, and make it through the day when there's nothing left in the tank. The problem with autopilot is that we aren't mindful of it. Instead, we sit back, put on the oxygen mask, and tell autopilot to do its thing. Unfortunately, autopilot mode isn't always the healthiest way of getting through life, nor is it the most enjoyable or peaceful. You see, autopilot only has one job and one job: Make it out alive. While staying alive is obviously great, as humans, we need to do more than just be alive; we need to live! To live requires you to get out of your comfort zone, change your mindset often, and be ambitious; all things that autopilot will never do.

Regarding confidence, your autopilot might be set up in "protection" mode, which means that whenever you have an awkward situation, your autopilot mode is to get the hell out of there! Autopilot might be screaming at you to leave mid-presentation and take a sick day, which isn't very confidence-building. That's why we need to take the plane out of autopilot mode if we want to remain confident in even the most awkward moments. However, how do we do that? How do we go from autopilot to, well, non-autopilot? The answer lies in Mindfulness.

According to the American Psychological Association (2022), Mindfulness is the "awareness of one's internal states and surroundings." Okay, yes, that sounds a little creepy, but it's actually a beautiful thing! When you are mindful, you become aware of everything you're feeling, why you feel that way, and how you can respond appropriately. It can also help you to avoid destructive habits and automatic responses. Say goodbye to autopilot! There are various ways in which you can improve your mindfulness. My personal favorite mindfulness technique is called a Body Scan. It's way less medical than it sounds, I promise!

### Body Scan

A Body Scan is a type of meditation that boosts mindfulness. In short, it's a method that helps you become aware of your feelings and be present in the moment. It lets you let go of fear and negative emotions, boosting confidence. Once you recognize your negative thoughts and feelings about yourself and your situation, you can do something about them. You can switch from autopilot mode to manual and decide how you want to react and respond. Personally, body scans have helped me to realize that the world doesn't always revolve around me. As cynical as it might sound, I believed everyone was always mad at me. If I saw someone with a slight frown or being different than usual in the smallest way possible, I would immediately assume that it's because of me. My autopilot response was to retreat into my shell, avoid everyone, and sit with self-pity for the rest of the day, believing that everyone hated me. Once I started practicing body scans, I recognized that I feared disappointing those around me; therefore, I always jumped to the conclusion that I already did something to upset people. I was able to recognize that Susan, the receptionist, is, in fact, not mad at me, but her car broke down on the way to work, and she isn't sure how she'll be able to afford the repairs while her house is under construction and her kids are in need of new school shoes. Recognizing that the world doesn't always revolve around me helped me to gain confidence in conversation because I no longer took everyone else's behavior as a direct reaction to my behavior. I started realizing that people have their own feelings and their own things that they are dealing with. Now, when I say "Hi" to Susan, and she doesn't respond like she usually does, I know that she has her own things to deal with, and it's not because of me. It gave me the confidence to continue the conversation because instead of making it about me, I knew that perhaps I could help her and improve her day. Now, let me walk you through a quick body scan.

1. Find a comfortable spot to sit or lay down, and close your eyes.
2. Become aware of your body as you relax every muscle.
3. Notice 5 things that you can hear.
4. Think about 3 things that you can feel.
5. Now, what are the 2 things that you can smell?

## HOW TO TALK TO ANYONE AT WORK | 65

6. What can you taste?
7. Next, think about your feet. Do you feel pain, pressure, or any other feeling in your feet? Then, focus on relaxing your feet.
8. Move up to your legs and follow the same questioning as you did in step seven. Move up through your whole body until you come to your head.
9. Breathe in deeply and exhale all the stress. Imagine peace and confidence rushing over your entire body as you exhale.
10. Let go of all negative thoughts about yourself and what you're currently experiencing.

Once you're done with your body scan, ask yourself some questions regarding your situation and try to answer them objectively. For example, I used to ask myself:

*Did you do anything to upset this person on purpose?*

*Is it in their character to tell you when they are upset?*

*Is it in their character to be passive-aggressive?*

*Can you control what they are feeling?*

*Is there something else going on in their lives?*

The body scan helped me relax and calm down my anxiety, which allowed me to answer the questions objectively and find that perhaps I wasn't the problem after all, which gave me the confidence to go about my day.

### A Few Other Options

If a body scan doesn't sound like your cup of tea, that's okay. However, Mindfulness doesn't just serve one cup of tea but an entire coffee shop of varieties. Here are a few other simple ways to practice mindfulness and keep your confidence (Roberts, 2013).

1. Go for a walk and, as you walk, become aware of your senses. Start to notice the temperature, the smells and scents, the people around you, the colors, and the situations. Find something unique that makes you smile.
2. When you're on your way to work, listen to music and focus on the instruments. Notice how it changes and builds. Become aware of how this changes your experience.
3. Use a guided meditation podcast where you follow along with the instructor.
4. Eat while using all of your senses. When we're on autopilot, we tend to eat our food without thinking. Be mindful of the taste, textures, and

feelings that come with the food. Focus on eating slowly and enjoying every bite.

5. To distract yourself from awkwardness, play a game in your head. For example, think of ten things that start with E or five cities that start with H. Give it a couple of minutes, and then evaluate whether your feelings of awkwardness are still strong.

You might read through these and think, "There's no way these simple tricks will boost my confidence!" Well, even if you currently have the self-confidence of a toad, I can guarantee that these small practices will help you. It might not happen overnight, and it might not give you enough self-confidence to step onto the stage and sing karaoke, but it will help you to survive the situation you're in with some dignity. These small mindfulness practices will help you to achieve a calmer state of mind. When you enter a stressful situation, your nervous system flares up, sending signals all over your body, screaming, "Code RED! People incoming!" When you take a moment to distract your mind with something else, allowing it to calm down, it forgets about "code red" and focuses on the task at hand. It's a little bit like a cute dog seeing a ball: As long as it focuses on the ball, it doesn't realize anything else is happening around them. So, in short, these mindfulness tricks are simply a distraction in one form or another, allowing your brain to take a couple of seconds to relax and forget that it was nervous in the first place.

## CUTTING NEGATIVE SELF-TALK

Earlier, we chatted a little about negative self-talk and the inner critic that tends to tear us apart for pleasure, so we already know how to identify the inner critic, but how do we cut it out completely? How can we go from negative self-talk to remaining confident when the pawpaw strikes the fan? The answer lies in intentionality. You have to intentionally replace your inner critic with your biggest fan. One of my dearest friends uses a method that she likes to call "The Bestie Method." Whenever she discovers her inner critic taking control, she stops and asks herself: Would I talk to my best friend this way? Usually, the answer is an immediate no. Just imagine for a quick second that your best friend is going for an interview at her dream organization. Then, just before she walks into the room, you pull her aside and whisper, "You're going to mess this up. You're not good enough for this job. Just saying." Not a great move as a friend, am I right? So, why do you do it to yourself? You can cut negative self-talk by constantly talking to yourself the way you would talk to your best friend. Sure, sometimes that means a little bit of tough love, but the emphasis is on the LOVE.

Being kinder to yourself is a wonderful way of cutting down negative self-talk. Start each day by writing down three kind things about yourself. It can be whatever comes into your mind, as long as it's kind and meaningful. Then, whenever negative self-talks emerge, focus on the kind things you wrote about yourself instead. Acceptance is another way of combating negative self-talk (Headspace, 2022). When you accept yourself for who you are and don't expect perfection, you'll find it easier to love yourself and remain confident when things go astray. Accept that you are human and will make mistakes, but also accept that you are magnificent, alive, and have so much to offer. Accept that you can be celebrated and successful and that the voices that tell you otherwise are lying. Accept that you have limitations and let go of everything you cannot control. Letting go of control is one of the most efficient ways of cutting out negative self-talk completely. Here's a quick step-by-step on what to do when you catch your inner critic (Scott, 2022).

1. Recognize the negative thoughts and that it is your inner critic speaking.
2. Remember that your feelings aren't always reality, and how you feel now will pass.

3. Contain your negativity about yourself by not saying it out loud or spreading it to someone else.
4. Remain calm and find your neutral point of view.
5. Ask the critic whether it's true or not. Examine the facts.
6. Replace it with something good and say it out loud.
7. Repeat until you feel better about yourself.

All of the above methods are great, especially for everyday use, but what happens when the rubber meets the road, and you desperately need confidence in a social situation? The following two methods focus on exactly that: Finding your confidence in a situation that screams awkwardness.


PREPARATION

Have you ever canceled an event or a social situation moments before you were supposed to leave because you simply didn't have enough willpower to deal with social encounters? Well, you're not alone, so there is literally no shame in that. However, did you know that recent studies show that willpower is, in fact, not really a thing? Before I lose you, hear me out. Studies have found that willpower is not something you have or don't have but rather something you can learn. It's grit. The good news is that you can train yourself to have more grit. The bad news is that you can no longer blame your cancellations on willpower. Jokes aside, though, it's actually a remarkable finding because knowing that you can train yourself to have grit means that you are in control. You're not relying on a personality trait that you feel you never received or waiting for some magical force to make you confident; you can train yourself to have "willpower" (Lund, 2021).

There are six types of grit, according to Steven Kotler, that you need in order to perform at your highest level (Lund, 2021):

- The grit to recover
- The grit to master your fears
- The grit to train your weakness
- The grit to persevere
- The grit to control your thoughts
- The grit to be your best when you are at your worst

According to Kotler, you need "the grit to train your pain" if you want to accomplish the other grits (Lund, 2021). It sounds terrible, kind of like some sort of torture method, but it's actually quite simple. It's the idea that you must practice doing things even when you don't feel like doing them. For example, practice talking to strangers, even if you really don't want to. Alternatively, practice going to social events, even if you might only know one person there. You have to develop the habit of doing what you don't want to do to make it less painful every time you do it. It's all about being prepared for when it's gameday.

When you don't want to do something, and things aren't in the optimal state, do it anyway. Why? Well, because things never go as planned, and the more prepared you are for the unpreparable, the more confident you'll be when things go awry. The best way to do that is to practice when things aren't in the optimal state. For example, let's say you've prepared to give a presentation that will take about 45 minutes, but due to technical difficulties, you only have 20 minutes. What will you do? Do you know which parts of the presentation you can cut out if need be? When you practice for the worst-case scenarios, you'll not only be prepared for if it happens, but you'll be able to remain calm and collected.

If you know there's a big function at the end of the year where you'll have to go on stage and deliver a speech, are you going to spend the entire year in agony, avoiding the inevitable, or are you going to take some steps and prepare? We're all tempted to do the first, but the latter is probably a much wiser decision. You can prepare by doing precisely what you don't want to do: Speaking in public. Start small. Give a speech at your anniversary dinner or your mom's birthday in front of other family members. Practice in front of the mirror. Do an online public speaking class and use the tips they provide. Give a presentation at work so you can get used to speaking in front of your colleagues. And then, get on that stage and be confident that you've prepared enough to make a success of the speech, regardless of who is watching.

## VISUALIZATION

Imagine you are at a work event. You spent almost an hour trying to follow a makeup tutorial which seemed way easier than it actually was, just to wash your face and start again midway through. You tried curling your hair with your straighter like you've seen other girls do flawlessly, yet somehow you were left with a frizzy mess. Luckily, you're a master of the quick updo using a few bobby pins. You tried on almost every outfit in your closet, just to realize that the one you had on first was the best. After two hours of excruciating decision-making, you put on your lucky shoes, grab your purse, and walk out the door, ready to network. You walk into the party just as you receive a message from your work best friend, letting you know that they won't be able to make it. You feel a little stressed. Who are you supposed to talk to now? You walk into the room anyway and see a hundred faces of people you don't know. You sprint towards the welcoming drinks, grab a glass of champagne, and stuff your mouth with a tiny chicken pie. As you turn around, you're greeted by your boss and, next to him, one of the biggest names in the industry. You try to swallow your chicken pie, but the heat overwhelms your throat. You consider spitting it out but quickly decide against it and try your best to swallow it down with some champagne while the two men stare at you, waiting for a response. How awkward, right?

What you just did is called visualization. You imagined something. However, did you know that how you imagine yourself to act and react is most likely to become true the next time you're at a social event? Crazy right? That's why you need to practice positive visualization. So, let's continue the previous image in a positive way.

You swallow your chicken pie and give a big smile. "That's why you should never work through lunch on the day of a gala," you say jokingly. The two men laugh as you shake their hands firmly, maintaining eye contact. You introduce yourself to the industry leader and compliment his work, showing that you know your story and whom you're talking to. You casually drop that you're working on something similar, leaving the conversation open to him. You chat for another few minutes while subtly complimenting your boss and the work environment he has created. As they walk away, you get the nod of approval from your boss and feel confident that you can talk to anyone. You spend the whole night networking and talking to other people in the industry. You leave sober, happy, and satisfied with the night's events.

When you visualize how something will go and how you will act, you expand your ability to relax and focus on the success that you can achieve. So before every social event, take a couple of moments to visualize how you'll be seen, how you'll act, and how confident you'll remain (Star, 2019).

Visualizations can be extremely helpful when preparing for big moments, like speaking in front of an audience. However, it's equally valuable when you have to engage in small talk. This next chapter is all about how you can master the art of small talk. Who knew that talking about the weather could actually be entertaining?

4

## MASTERING SMALL TALK

When I was in my early twenties, I started working in an office with about twenty other people. We had a vivacious office culture filled with birthday celebrations, casual Fridays, and extended coffee breaks to talk about the weather and the latest celebrity gossip. It sounds great, right? Well, it was a bit much for someone with social anxiety, to be quite honest with you. Like, no, Brenda, I don't want to see photos of your cats, your grandkids, or your grandkids holding your cats because I will have no idea how to get out of the conversation and continue my work. Anyway, we had a staff meeting every Wednesday in the boardroom (which had swings for chairs, by the way). And every week, like clockwork, my boss would be ten minutes late for said meeting. Now, ten minutes might not sound like much, except if you're exercising or socially awkward and need to make small talk. However, you see, I also couldn't wait for my boss before I entered the boardroom. We had to be seated at 10 am SHARP! My hands would get sticky, my breathing would quicken as if I just ran up a flight of stairs, and I would start sweating like a racehorse. And then my mind would start spinning...

What will we talk about?

What if I'm awkward?

What if I spoil the season finale of Stranger Things for someone who hasn't watched it yet?

Or worse, what if I insult Brenda's cat (or grandchild)?

It was only years later that I cracked the code of small talk. Want to know my biggest finding? My mindset was wrong, and my actions showed it. I spent so much time trying to avoid small talk that I completely missed the importance and impact of small talk on relationships. It wasn't just a case of confidence but a case of "I don't deem small talk important, so I refuse to engage." The truth is that small talk is incredibly important in relationship building, networking, and making a good impression.

In this chapter, we'll talk some more about small talk, the importance of it, and how we can master it to ensure that conversation doesn't stop at small talk but evolves into deeper, meaningful conversations.

## THE SMALL TALK MINDSET

If you relate to the story of me and the belated meetings, you might think of small talk and immediately start feeling awkward. That's okay! Trust me, it took a long time and a lot of effort to change my perspective on small talk, but it's possible, and it all starts by changing your mindset. One of the biggest reasons people fear small talk is because they feel like they have nothing to talk about. I recently watched the Netflix series Crown (if you don't want spoilers, look away!), which follows the story of the British royals. In one particular episode, Queen Elizabeth II gets herself a tutor because she is afraid that she has nothing to talk about with the foreign politicians and leaders. She feels that her upbringing failed her and that she can't hold her own in conversation. Later in the episode, her tutor helps her realize that she knows a lot about various topics, especially where her input is required the most. Now, if you're wondering what this has to do with you, you might be surprised to find that most of us aren't that different from the Queen in this regard. We often fear conversation because, "What if it's awkward?" or, "What if we have nothing to talk about?" I want you to take a deep breath and know this: No matter who you are, you know a lot of things. Whether it's about your profession, your college major, your network, or simply your unique point of view (Olivia, 2020), the knowledge you carry can benefit those around you or at least tickle their curiosity for a moment or two. Let this sink in.

***You are valuable.***

Once you believe that you have something of value to contribute to the conversation, making small talk will immediately feel less daunting. Socializing is not about controlling the conversation and having it all planned out, but rather a way of collaborating with others, trading knowledge and wisdom. The best way to start such social transactions is by engaging in small talk. Do you see? It's not just a time-filling conversation; it's the building blocks that lead to deeper relationships.

To get into the small talk mindset, there are three things that you need to remind yourself of constantly, or at least until the idea of small talk doesn't come with a dose of sweaty armpits and a racing heart.

## HOW TO TALK TO ANYONE AT WORK | 81

### You Are the Host

Tell yourself that you are the host of the conversation. Just as sports players perform better (mostly) when playing on their home turf, tell yourself that this is your home court. You have the advantage. So, be proactive and ask questions. Jump into the conversation with confidence and a smile that reaches the eyes (Olivia, 2020). If you're at an event, ask the person, "What do you think about the event so far?" as if you're the one who organized it. I can guarantee you that this will make you feel more confident immediately!

### This Won't Kill Me

A study that was conducted in 2007 found that humans feel the same amount of stress in social situations, as primates do when they run away from predators (Stanford University, 2007). Meaning we're so scared of social encounters that we literally act as if we might die. Well, ask yourself, what's the worst that can happen? Sure, you could make a joke, and the other person might not laugh, or someone might ask you something you don't know the answer to, but so what? Having one awkward conversation won't kill you and won't affect your career. Life will continue as it is right now. A good conversation can boost you forward, but making one awkward joke with someone you'll probably never see again, usually won't do much damage. So if you get nervous, just remember that small talk won't kill you.

### Future Friends

Okay, this might sound like the beginning of a sad coming-of-age movie where the girl's only friend is her mom, but I promise you that it will boost your confidence! Before you enter small talk, tell yourself that this person you're about to talk to is your best friend whom you haven't met yet. Going into the conversation with the idea that this person is a friend, an ally, and someone close to you will not only make you feel more confident, but it will also stop you from judging the person harshly. Remember, in many cases, the person you're trying to talk to is equally as nervous as you are (Olivia, 2020).

Okay, now that you've got the small talk mindset, let's look at some small talk topics you should embrace and some you should probably try to avoid.

## SMALL TALK TOPICS

Since most people fear "What will we talk about?" when it comes to small talk, let's fix that! Preparation is the key to confidence, after all. There are a couple of topics you should probably avoid when talking to someone for the first time, like that story about when you had

HOW TO TALK TO ANYONE AT WORK | 83

head lice and had to shave your head. Maybe save that for later. Much, much later. Before we examine the topics you should avoid, though, let's look at the topics you should entertain. Warning, it's not life-changing stuff. Small talk will lead to a deeper conversation where you can have the life-changing stuff, but if you jump right in with global warming, you might put the other person off. Rather stick to these if you're unsure.

### How's the Weather?

As mundane and tedious as it might sound, talking about the weather is great for small talk! It's a neutral topic with very, very little possibility of offending anyone. Think about the weather you're currently experiencing. Is there a storm about to blow through? Are you experiencing the heat wave of the century? Use it as a small talk conversation starter (Cuncic, 2022)!

- I absolutely love spring. Such a beautiful day, don't you think?
- This rain is crazy! I almost lost my umbrella on the way in. *insert polite laughter here*
- What a glorious evening. Just what I ordered.

Although the above might sound funny now, in social environments, it works perfectly to engage in small talk. If you find yourself with awkward silence between conversations, bring up the weather, and you'll see everyone will have something to say.

### I Love That Movie!

Arts and entertainment topics are great conversation starters (Cuncic, 2022). Use things like movies, television shows, popular music, or books to engage in small talk, and invite the other person to share what they love with you. For example:

- Are you reading any good books at the moment? I could really use some recommendations.
- This new podcast I started listening to is golden! What types of podcasts do you enjoy?
- Are you also on the Candy Crush bandwagon? So am I! How did you defeat level 315?

State everything as a question to avoid talking about books or movies that the other person hasn't read or watched yet. If no one has watched the movie, don't continue the conversation with a reference from said movie. It will only make you feel awkward, and no one will laugh with you. Remember, small talk is about practice, so if the conversation leads nowhere, that's also okay (Cuncic, 2022). Also, make sure you try a different topic next time you talk to the same people.

### Can You Believe They Won?

Sports is my go-to topic when talking to people I don't know very well. Whenever I feel the conversation is about to die, I throw in some sports reference, and voilà! Conversation revived! Try these topics regarding the sport.

- I can't believe the Lions won. Did you watch the game?
- I'll probably die before they win again, but I'll always be a _____ fan! How about you?
- Who's your top draft pick for this season's NBA?

If you don't know anything about the sport, don't use sport as a conversation starter because chances are they will continue the conversation and ask you some questions in return. Oef, awkward.

### My Precious Family

Just as Brenda showed me pictures of her cats and her grandkids almost every day, most people love talking about their families. Brenda was actually allowing me to be part of her personal life. Instead of finding it awkward, I could've reciprocated by showing her some photos of my new puppy or my brother's newborn. Talking about your family is a great way to keep the conversation flowing without any awkwardness (Cuncic, 2022). Conversation starters about family can include:

- Do you have any siblings?
- How old are your kids now?
- Where did you grow up?

Remember, whatever you ask will probably come right back to you. So don't ask about a topic you don't want to share. Also, avoid sensitive questions like, "Why don't you have any children?" If the person brings up a family member, it's safe to assume that you may proceed with asking questions about that family member.

### I Love to Eat

Talking about food is a wonderful way of keeping the conversation going. People love talking about what they eat and don't eat, and bonus, you can keep your answers as short or complicated as you want.

- What's your favorite restaurant to go to?
- Do you cook at home often?
- I'm entirely out of lunchbox ideas. Any recommendations?

Stick with positive topics and avoid complaining about the food of the event you're attending. You never know who might hear you and take offense.

### How's the Overtime?

If you're at a work event, talking about work is probably the most common topic you'll encounter. If you're meeting new people in the industry, take the opportunity to ask them what they do, what they like about their job, and ask for their business cards. It's a great way of showing that you like them and that you care. Try using the following as conversation starters:

- How long have you worked at _____?
- What do you love the most about your job?
- How did you get into your line of work?

Focus on what you can learn from the other person (Cuncic, 2022). This will make the small talk conversations fun and valuable; however, remember that you're not interviewing the other person. So listen and keep it easy. Don't focus too much on the agenda.

### I've Been There!

If you enjoy traveling and have recently taken a trip, don't be scared to bring it up in conversation. Be sure to follow it with questions for the other person; otherwise, you might seem as if you're bragging about all your travels. You can ask the other person about their favorite traveling destinations, if they've ever been out of the country, and if they could go anywhere, where they would want to go (Cuncic, 2022). If you have a funny story about a country you and the other person visited, share it joyfully.

### I Adore Pottery

Hobbies make for great conversation starters. If you feel like you don't have any hobbies, ask for recommendations or tips on starting a new hobby. Chances are that the other person will love sharing their hobby with you and try to convince you to start doing it immediately (Cuncic, 2022). As the other person is speaking, listen and ask follow-up questions regarding their hobby. For example, if someone says something like, "I haven't painted in ages," ask them why and if they would like to paint more in the coming weeks.

### Small Town Things

When you talk about your hometown, it feels personal, even though it isn't really. So, use that warm and fuzzy feeling and engage with others about their hometowns. For example:

- Did you enjoy growing up in _____?

- Do you live a lot differently now than you did growing up?
- What do you miss the most about _____?

Have a funny or interesting story about your hometown ready, and if the opportunity arises, break the ice with your story. Who knows, perhaps someone can relate or grew up similarly to you.

### She Said What?

Celebrity gossip is always a fun topic to engage with. The best part is that you don't really have to be up to date with celebrity news to engage. However, maybe don't try and gossip about Taylor Swift to your boss. Rather keep the celebrity talk for a more informal and casual party and not a formal work event where you're supposed to be networking for new clients.

Now that you have ten topics you can use for small talk, here are the ten topics you should avoid, like the plague, unless specifically brought up by the other person (Cuncic, 2022).

- finances
- politics and religion
- sex
- death
- appearance

- personal gossip
- offensive jokes
- narrow topics
- past relationships
- health

## IT'S NOT AS BAD AS IT SOUNDS

As someone who used to struggle with severe anxiety, I understand that we tend to make things worse in our minds than they really are. It's not a fun fact to admit, but it's the truth. It's one of the many symptoms of anxiety, depression, and intrusive thoughts; struggling to see what is true and what your mind has made into a bigger mountain than it actually is. The truth is, when you have social anxiety, it's not much different. Not entirely sure what I mean? Let me tell you this story about Sarah.

Sarah is one of my best friends in the world. We worked together for a couple of years; however, our friendship started out slow. It definitely wasn't a "friends at first sight" scenario. In fact, I found her a little annoying at first, and she thought I was a loner who stayed in his mom's basement (her words, not mine). We kind of avoided each other for the first couple of months after we met for entirely different reasons. I thought I offended her when we first met because I didn't offer to buy her a coffee while I got coffee for everyone else in the office. I didn't leave her out on purpose; I just didn't know her coffee order, and asking her felt like too much of a social interaction, so I just left it (not a cool move, I know).

On the other hand, she avoided me because she bumped into me while I was carrying a tray of coffees, causing me to spill a couple of them onto my crisp white shirt. To be honest, I can't even remember doing that! I'm so used to being clumsy that I didn't blame her for even a second, while she couldn't even remember that I didn't get her a coffee because she doesn't even drink coffee (I try not to hold that against her). You see what I'm getting at? We avoided each other like the plague because we both thought we offended or upset the other person when in reality, we didn't care. We were so obsessed with our own behavior that we didn't even notice each other's behavior.

How often do you think we do that? We're so convinced that the other person must have a bad first impression of us that we just don't ever approach them again. It's quite scary when you think about it. We just assume that the other person is thinking about us and our awkward small talk when in reality, they couldn't really care less. Let me tell you a secret: Other people don't think about you as often as you fear. When you're lying awake at night, remembering that time you made a joke, and no one laughed, others can't even remember. When Sarah and I finally talked (because we were assigned to the same project), we realized that we actually had a lot in common (except for the coffee drinking). We finally shared our initial fears about our first encounter and had a proper laugh. We were so self-absorbed when the other person literally didn't even remember what we feared so much.

See this as a reminder not to overthink when small talk doesn't go your way. Remember, this isn't a Christmas movie where every cute thing we say and every quirk we have gets remembered (or even seen) by the other person. In most cases, the other person didn't even notice or will forget in two minutes tops. And in any case, if you try your best to keep a conversation going and it still falls flat, consider the idea that it's not your fault. Perhaps the other person is just terrible at small talk and secretly envies your confidence and small talk skills.

Even when you crash and burn, it's not really that bad, and you'll be okay if you manage not to take that as a sign to stop trying.

## FROM SMALL TALK TO BIG TALK

While small talk is necessary to build the initial foundations of a connection, deeper conversation (or as I like to call it, Big Talk) is required to build deeper connections. So, how do we go from "What's your favorite color?" to "My dream is to write a best-selling novel"? How do we start with, "I went to Bali once," and move into conversations that flow easily? You know, those conversations where you are past small talk, but you're not quite ready to share your deep, dark secrets just yet. Well, it's actually not as complicated as you might think. Let's start with the basics (Charisma on Command, 2017).

### *Compliment and Cold Read*

Okay, so you're in the conversation, and you've covered a couple of the topics we discussed earlier. Now what? Well, one way to keep the conversation fun and engaging is by giving a compliment, followed by a cold read. A cold read is simply a guess about the person's life, which fits with the compliments. For example, if the person has made you laugh twice already, you can say, "Wow, you're hilarious. Are you a comedian?" (Charisma on Command, 2017). You see? That's a compliment, plus a cold read. The best part is that even if you're wrong, the other person will feel flattered and be much more likely to engage in the conversation further. In this case, they'll probably start talking about what they actually do for a living (Charisma on Command, 2017).

### An Avalanche of Words

When you're new at small talk, asking questions is a great way to communicate. The problem, however, is that a lot of questions can quickly start to feel like an interrogation, or worse, an impromptu interview. This can be avoided by asking something that will get the other person talking and talking and talking, like an avalanche of words (Charisma on Command, 2017). Try to avoid asking questions that require one-word responses. For example, instead of asking, "How's work going?" ask, "What's new and exciting at work?" Instead, find something that the other person is passionate about and allow them to get excited and word vomit a little bit. This will make the person feel that you care about their life and give you a break from talking.

### Game Time

If you're bored with typical small talk, turn it into a game. For example, instead of asking the person where they're from and waiting for their answer, ask them for three clues and then take a guess (Charisma on

Command, 2017). This will get the other person thinking and speaking, and it will be fun and more relaxing than an interrogating question. It doesn't matter if you guess right or not; the whole point is to just connect on a fun level and build a relationship with the other person.

# PAYING IT FORWARD

*"The more I help others to succeed, the more I succeed."* — *Ray Kroc*

There's a lot of information here, and an important part of any journey – whether it's a 10-mile hike or a quest to improve your confidence and communication skills – is taking a break.

In fact, taking short breaks is key to learning! It allows us to consolidate the information we've taken in, enabling us to put it into practice more effectively.

In this instance, it also gives us a moment to reflect. Our journey started with the importance of good communication, and it's through deepening my own understanding of this that I came to be here, communicating with you through my writing.

My goal is to help those plagued by social anxiety and lacking in confidence to overcome the struggles that I have faced myself... and as your own confidence improves, I'd hazard a guess that you'll feel a pull to help others too.

You have an opportunity to start right now!

**By leaving a review of this book on Amazon, you'll show new readers that they're not alone – and exactly where they can find the information that will help them improve their confidence and communication skills.**

Simply by letting other readers know how this book has helped you and what they can expect to find inside, you'll help more people find the route to improving their confidence – and as a result, live far happier and less stressful lives.

I know how difficult social anxiety can be, and it's my goal to help as many people as I can to overcome it. Thank you for your support – I couldn't do this without you!

## 5

# BUILDING RELATIONSHIPS

When I first started my journey of becoming a better communicator, I was determined quite literally to put every single thing that I read into practice. I thought I was doing great! I was talking to more people, giving myself small pats on the back when I did something that scared me, and suddenly felt much more talkative than before. Here's how I thought I looked:

I believed that I was Harvey Specter from the hit television series Suits. Let me paint you a picture if you're unfamiliar with this character. He's confident and a little cocky, but not too much. He's funny and charming when he wants to be, can converse with anyone, and demands attention when he enters the room. He has a swaggering walk which screams confidence! He makes great eye contact; his body language is always calm and collected; above all, people love him (when he wants them to). I truly thought I was becoming more and more like Harvey Specter. Do you want to know what I *actually* looked like, however?

Sheldon Cooper from another hit television series, The Big Bang Theory. His robotic way of doing life, especially when he learns a new skill, makes for great television but for a terrible colleague.

I was so focused on applying everything I learned that I came across as manipulative, robotic, and somehow more awkward than before. Now, I'm not telling you this to freak you out and stop you from practically implementing these tools. I just want to help you not make the same mistake I did. I forgot something fundamental: I forgot to listen. I missioned through my list of "how to be cool" and ended up not hearing anything the other person said. Instead of building relationships, I pushed people away. I wouldn't be surprised to learn that people hid in closets and printing rooms to avoid me. It wasn't pretty, but it was salvageable. As Sarah kindly pointed out, "Turn down the thinking, dude."

As tempted as I was never to speak again, I learned that having healthy work relationships is incredibly important if you want to be a success, so I had to swallow my pride, hide my embarrassment, and try again. That's what this chapter is all about: Finding the balance within relationship building with colleagues. We'll talk about why it's important to have good relationships with co-workers, how to go from acquaintances to work friends, and how to influence others without manipulating them. Let's get right into it to prevent you from having your very own Sheldon Cooper moment.

## THE IMPORTANCE OF HEALTHY WORK RELATIONSHIPS

Imagine for a second that you just landed your dream job…

You have a corner office that you don't have to share with anyone else, an extraordinary view, and a big stationary budget so you can get all the sticky notes your heart desires. You even have a mini fridge under your desk, stocked daily with fresh water and your favorite soft drinks. There's a Nespresso coffee machine with unlimited pods, and you are "forced" to take an hour lunch every day. You get paid double for overtime, and you have the weekends off. Did I mention they also pay for your transport to work and back? Everything is perfect, but there's a catch: The people suck. They're all stuck-up, loud, and obnoxious. They don't allow you to speak in meetings, they don't greet you in the morning, and they often call you "girly" because they can't remember your name. They have parties and invite everyone but you, and they blame you for things they failed to do. Oh, and they heat their tuna casserole in the lunch area, which stinks up the whole place. Your dream job quickly turned into a nightmare, right?

That's because work relationships hugely impact how much you enjoy your job and job satisfaction. According to Shauna Waters, professor, author, and leadership coach, if you have a solid relationship with your colleagues, you'll be much more likely to enjoy going to work and be more efficient (Waters, 2022). Human connection is undeniably one of the most needed things any person requires to thrive; just think about how the pandemic influenced people's human connection and mental health. However, building strong work relationships takes time and effort, and it might cause you to stop and think: "Is this really worth it?"

The answer is yes! Take a moment and think about how much time you spend at work. More or less eight hours a day, five times a week, which is more or less 160 hours a month... That's a lot of time to spend with people you don't like. When you have healthy work relationships, you will have more respect for your coworkers, and they will have more respect for you.

Now, if you think having your coworkers' respect isn't that important, just talk to someone who's worked in a toxic environment, and you'll see just how important it is. Teams who don't trust each other will struggle to be productive, creating poor team culture. Studies have also shown that a poor work environment can lead to mental health problems and can contribute to burnout (Waters, 2022).

Let me paint another picture for you: It's been a long year, and every day feels like a struggle. You're running on copious amounts of caffeine and wishful thinking. Lucky for you, your leave got approved, meaning that you are on your way to Bali for a 10-day vacation on the beach! You spend your week catching some good sun, sleeping in, swimming, drinking cocktails, and reading the book that's been on your nightstand the entire year. You've never felt so relaxed in your life! Your headaches are gone, your posture is better, and you're even getting along with your in-laws for once. As you return from your holiday, you're determined to maintain your relaxation, so you get into bed early, feeling prepared to get back to work and show off your new tan. However, as your alarm clock goes off, you feel a tsunami of stress rush over you. You're struggling to breathe, your headache is pounding, and the outfit you chose for the day seems wrong. You feel anxious just thinking about walking into the office, and you start contemplating calling in sick. You can't understand why. Last night you were perfectly fine, but now you're feeling panicked, and work hasn't even started yet! Have you ever experienced something similar?

This isn't because your holiday wasn't long or relaxing enough. It's because burnout isn't just a result of being overworked, despite what most people think. There are actually six things that trigger burnout (Waters, 2022):

1. Lack of control
2. Conflict in values
3. Insufficient reward
4. Work overload
5. Unfairness
6. Community breakdown

Yes, that's right. Your community can cause you to have burnout. Still don't think the right colleagues and work environment are important? Working with patronizing, rude, or simply toxic colleagues can lead to you experiencing burnout and anxiety, just like the example I gave. It's essential for your mental health to have positive work relationships. Despite seeming impossible, positive work relationships are completely obtainable and very beneficial to you, your colleagues, and your employer. Here are some of the benefits of positive work relationships (Waters, 2022):

- It increases job satisfaction, meaning people are less likely to quit or change industries.
- It's way less awkward during meetings and improves innovation since no one is scared to speak up.
- You'll get more support from your colleagues when going through a stressful situation at work or home. Good colleagues will always step in to take something off your plate.

If you're wondering now whether you have a good relationship with your colleagues or not, here are a few signs that you are in good work relationships (Waters, 2022):

- You and your colleagues trust each other.
- There's mutual respect between everyone.
- Everyone is involved in decision-making, not just the top dogs.
- Everyone is honest and open with each other.

## HOW TO BUILD GOOD RELATIONSHIPS WITH COLLEAGUES

Now that we know that having good work relationships is important and that warming your tuna casserole in the shared lunch room should be illegal, it's time to look at how we can practically build good relationships with our colleagues. As we all know, it's one thing to know something and a completely different story to actually do something about it. As a socially awkward introvert prone to clumsiness and foot-in-mouth syndrome, I was terrified of building relationships with colleagues. So, I constantly told myself that it would naturally happen over time. Well, I gave myself plenty of time, and you know what happened? Not much. Sure, my colleagues got more comfortable with me, and I with them, but that's kind of it. I would wait until everyone was finished at the coffee station before refilling my cup, while others would go together to catch up on weekend plans and discuss upcoming projects. Although it pains me deeply to admit this, it hurt my feelings a little bit. I felt like the middle school kid who always got picked last for team sport, but it was all my own doing. As soon as I started practicing these principles that I'm about to share with you, everything changed. Don't be like me and wait for next year to build better relationships with your colleagues. Start today and take it from there. According to Waters, you can do nine things to build better relationships with your colleagues. Let's have a look.

### What Do You Want?

One of my wife's favorite movies is the Nicholas Sparks hit, The Notebook. She has made me watch it about a dozen times, and I can probably recite the entire script by heart now. I've noticed one scene in particular that makes my wife melt. You probably know the scene I'm talking about already, right? Yes, the one where they're outside, and Noah passionately yells at Allie, "What do you want?" Who knew that all a woman desires every now and then is to know that someone wants her to put herself first? Anyway, when you're building a relationship with your coworkers, you need to ask yourself what you want. What does your ideal team look like? Do you want to be invited to weekend get-togethers outside of work? You need to know what you want from your colleagues because that will influence how you interact with them. You should also consider what your colleagues might want from you. Are you the only one in the office with a swimming pool in the middle of a heatwave? Then don't mention it if you're not planning on inviting them over to cool off a little.

Think about what you want out of the relationship and ask yourself what it is that you can also offer them. It needs to go both ways if you want the relationship to continue.

### Actually Listen!

By now, you know that it's important to practice active listening. If you don't want to end up like me in my robotic era, then you should probably listen to what the other person is saying before asking a follow-up question. Trust and communication skills are the foundations of a healthy relationship, and the best way to achieve that is by active listening (Waters, 2022). Use nonverbal communication to show that you're listening and actually care about what they're saying. The fastest way to lose relationships with people is not to listen when they're talking. If someone can't trust that you'll listen to them when they speak, they won't share what they're feeling and definitely won't invite you to help them brainstorm on a new project (Waters, 2022). On the other hand, once your teammates know that you listen when they speak, relationships will start to form naturally.

### Make Time

You can't build a relationship if you never spend time together. Make sure that you spend enough time with your colleagues, even when your schedule is busy. Invite someone to walk with you when you're quickly going to grab a coffee, or take some time to spend lunch together and talk (Waters, 2022). Spending time together will create space to build the relationship further. Even if you work remotely, have a virtual catch-up by scheduling a virtual coffee with a colleague. Be intentional with getting to know your colleagues and building your work relationship.

### Be Committed

Part of relationship building is helping others out, and the fastest way to destroy a relationship is by not sticking to your commitments. If you promised to help a colleague with a specific task, then you better stick to that commitment. Don't be the person that says, "Sure, I'll help as soon as I get the chance," and then is never heard from again. Helping colleagues meet their deadlines will prove that you're a reliable teammate, which will help build relationships (Waters, 2022). Before you demand that someone help you, offer to help someone else and show that you're committed to the team's success.

### Ask For Help

A big part of relationship building is showing that you trust those who work with you. Doing everything alone will hurt your credibility as a team player, so ask others for help and their opinion (Waters, 2022). Now that doesn't mean that you delegate all your work to others, but rather nicely ask a colleague to take something small off your plate when you feel overwhelmed. This is actually a popular method called *The Benjamin Franklin effect* (Shatz, 2022). In his autobiography, Benjamin Franklin describes how he dealt with the animosity of a rival legislator. Franklin heard that the rival had a very rare book in his private library, so he wrote to the rival, asking if he could borrow the book. The rival agreed, and after a week or so, Franklin returned the book with a note expressing his gratitude towards the rival. The next time they met, the rival spoke to Franklin with civility and continued to show a willingness to help him. Franklin summarized the events by saying, "He that has once done you a kindness will be more ready to do another than he whom you yourself have obliged." Asking your colleagues for help can be incredibly beneficial for your work relationship.

There's this multiplayer game that some of our couple of friends enjoy playing called It Takes Two. The premise is that you're a couple on the brink of divorce who gets trapped in the bodies of small wooden and clay figures that your child made. Together you have to face a series of obstacles, from fighting a vacuum cleaner to dealing with a wasp infestation. The key is that you have to do everything together with **collaboration**. Why am I telling you this? No, it's not so that you can play the game yourself (although I would highly recommend it). Rather, you understand the importance of collaboration. When you work together with someone to achieve the same goal, your relationship will grow stronger.

### Set Boundaries

Boundaries are incredibly important in building relationships with colleagues (Waters, 2022). Not only should you have boundaries, but you should also respect the other person's boundaries at all times. Striking that balance between a "healthy relationship" and "socializing too much" can be challenging, but it's not impossible. Remember that at the end of the day, these people are your colleagues, and you are still at work. So when you really need to focus and Charles can't stop chatting to you about his weekend plans, politely tell him that you're super interested in his story, but you really need to focus now. A time-blocking strategy can help you prioritize your tasks throughout the day, leaving enough space to still socialize and build relationships (Waters, 2022).

### Show Gratitude

"A little goes a long way in showing appreciation," says Waters (2022). You can show your teammates that you care about them by doing something small, like complimenting their work, getting them a snack when they're super busy, or celebrating their birthday in the office. Praise never goes unnoticed, especially when it's meant with a genuine heart, and it will positively impact your relationship. Even when you don't feel super grateful, try to maintain a positive outlook and don't rain on their parade. If someone has let you down, try to focus on what they did right and take it from there. A harsh word in a moment of anger can destroy all the progress you've made in that particular relationship. Be sure to give specific praise, not just a generalized nod of appreciation.

Imagine for a moment that you pulled an all-nighter to create the most beautiful and effective PowerPoint slide show that your office has ever seen. You didn't even mind the tiredness and red eyes when you walked into the office this morning because you felt so proud and confident of your presentation. You also spent hours practicing the presentation, knowing you would ace it! During the presentation, everything went perfectly! People laughed when they had to, went "ahh" at the moments you planned it, and made notes when you said something profound. You calmly also answered every question they had and presented yourself confidently! Now, of the two options below, what would make you feel better?

1. After the clients leave, your boss calls from across the boardroom, "Good job!" and walks away.

2. Your boss walks up to you, gives you a
   handshake, and says, "This was incredible.
   Thank you for being so prepared and taking
   great care of this presentation. I can see you
   spent hours making this slideshow, and it
   shows! The clients are blown away, and so am I.
   Great job!"

In both cases, the boss noticed your hard work and excellent presentation, but in scenario two, he specifically mentioned what you did right and praised you for those things. So, which one do you prefer? Probably the second one, right? Most people would because it feels good to get praised for specific things we do. So, next time you give a compliment at work, be specific and praise your colleagues for the things they paid attention to.

### Skip the Gossip

I know, a little harmless office gossip is always fun, especially on a Monday morning when you really don't want to be there, but it can cause a lot of damage in a relationship. Avoid talking behind people's backs, and always respect your colleagues (Waters, 2022). If you have a problem with someone, confront them directly and talk things out rather than spread gossip. Truth be told, the only reason we tend to spread gossip is to get validation from others, but it never works. When you're the one spreading the gossip, you're the one that cannot be trusted.

### Talk to Everyone

Finally, talk to and include everyone. Not just the manager who can put in a good word for you to get that promotion, but even the interns. When you only talk to the people you deem "important," it won't go unnoticed and will damage your relationship with others. Be friendly, kind, and open to all your colleagues, no matter their title or what they can get you. Theodore Roosevelt is the perfect example of putting this into practice. All his staff adored him, and his valet even wrote a book called *Theodore Roosevelt, Hero to His Valet*. His valet, James Amos, wrote that Roosevelt knew every single employee by name. Amos's wife, Annie, once asked Roosevelt about a bobwhite, a bird that was known to be in their region. She asked Roosevelt what it looked like because she had never seen one before in her life. He happily described the bird to her and continued with his day. A couple of weeks later, Amos received a phone call from Roosevelt, telling him that he spotted a bobwhite near their cottage on his morning walk and that Amos should tell Annie to look out the kitchen window. Small things like this made every employee feel seen by

Roosevelt. He even knew the gardener and the scullery maid, and he made a point to always greet everyone by their names (Carnegie, 1913). We can learn a great deal from Roosevelt in this regard. Instead of thinking that someone is below us or too young or unimportant, take a moment and really talk to them. It might do a lot more good than you anticipated.

## INFLUENCE VS. MANIPULATION

As I transformed from a socially awkward being to mastering small talk, I realized that I was quite afraid of engaging in deeper conversation. After my little robotics moment, I was scared that I would unknowingly manipulate people into liking me and acting advantageously toward me instead of influencing them to listen to my ideas. Somewhere along the way, the lines between influence and manipulation became blurry, and I was so scared of becoming a master manipulator instead of a master communicator. My thoughts began spiraling. What if I come across as inauthentic? What if they consider me cold and calculated? This spiraling led me to research the difference between influence and manipulation. Although many articles I read made me feel like there was no difference, one statement in one article really hit me. It was an article written by Clint Clarkson that said, "When we influence, we take the time to understand the needs of others and to fill those needs" (Clarkson, 2020). That was the first time I started seeing influence as a positive thing and not something to be scared of.

I started looking back at my life and the people who influenced me the most. Sure, there were a couple of negative influences, like that redhead John who influenced me to skip school when I was in high school. However, the majority of the influences were positive, like my dad, who influenced me to set up a savings account when I started my first job, or my mom, who influenced me to buy my wife flowers after she had a terrible week and my friends who influenced me to get out of my comfort zone which led me to meet my beautiful wife in the first place. I also had colleagues who influenced me positively. Do you remember Sarah from earlier? She influenced me to be more confident, while one of my other colleagues influenced me to work harder. So, how did they do it? How could they communicate effectively and influence me without being manipulative? After analyzing their behavior and doing additional research on the matter, I found four essential ways to influence them without manipulating them. Let's take a closer look at these four ways.

*Have Understanding*

If you want to avoid coming across as calculated and manipulative, you need to have an understanding of the person you're talking to. You need to understand who they are, how they normally communicate, and your relationship with them. If you don't have an understanding of the person, you'll be less invested in who they are and more interested in what they can do for you. Understand what the other person values and remain within their boundaries. For example, if Alex is a vegan, don't try to influence him to go on a hunting trip with you in an attempt to build a deeper connection with him. Have an understanding of the person and what they might currently be going through. For example, if Mary is going through a divorce, maybe don't talk about the wedding you went to the previous weekend in detail during a one-on-one conversation with her. When you better understand who the person is and what they're currently going through, you'll be more considerate and less manipulative.

*Establish Trust*

The second skill you need to influence and not manipulate is to establish trust. Without trust in the relationship, it won't grow into a mutually influencing partnership. If the other person doesn't trust you because of some past experience and you try to convince them to do something that will be beneficial, they might take that as intimidation and not as an influence. Make sure that there is a bond of mutual trust between you and the other person before you try and convince them to do something you'll benefit from. Trust is established through consistency and intentionality. People who don't trust you won't allow you to influence them (Jolles, 2020).

### Gain Commitment

If you want to influence someone, it requires their commitment. Unfortunately, few people wake up ready and committed to a new change (Jolles, 2020). If you're proposing a change in how things are being done in that person's life, you first need to ensure they are committed. In order to have commitment, you need to have a moment of truth with the other person. I had my moment of truth when Sarah told me that I was being weird and all "Sheldon Cooper" like. Because I trusted Sarah at that stage, she was able to influence me. I was committed to the cause because I trusted her insight. Before you attempt to influence someone, get them on board with the mission and the vision to ensure that you are equally committed.

### Mutually Beneficial Goal

The fourth thing you need to have to influence and not manipulate is a shared, mutually beneficial goal. The trick is that the goal must also be beneficial for the person you're trying to influence, not just for you. If it's only beneficial for you and you're trying to make the other person believe that they need it, that's manipulation. Let's say, for example, that you've just been tasked with a new project, but you're really not sure how you'll be able to manage it. It's quite a big task, and you'll need to sharpen your programming skills before starting. You really don't have the time and would love to pawn it off to someone else. You know that John has been under crossfire lately due to a minor mishap with a client who lost the company the deal, and you think he would be able to redeem himself with this new project. So, you approach John with a plan. "John, you are so much better at programming than I am. I think this project would be perfect for you since you also have tons of experience with databases which I don't have a clue about. Would you mind taking over this project? I would appreciate it so much, and I know you'll hit it out of the park." Giving the project to John is beneficial for you and John. You get to focus on everything you need to do already, while he can use this as an opportunity to show that he is valuable and good at what he does. If you don't want to pawn the whole project off to someone else, have a first attempt and then ask someone to review it. Offer to buy them a coffee to say thank you or sit next to them and work together to solve the problem. Be sure to give them credit and make them feel appreciated.

There you have it: have understanding, establish trust, gain commitment, and establish mutually beneficial goals. Now that you've mastered the art of transforming small talk into big talk, to make our conversations and relationships more meaningful, up next, we need to learn one of the trickiest things: How to keep and captivate someone's attention during conversation.

6

# CONNECT AND CAPTIVATE WITH STORIES

The warm carpet made me feel itchy as I sat with my legs crossed in front of my grandpa's rocking chair. His arms were resting on his big belly as he threw back his head, laughing at his own joke. A choir of giggles followed, every grandkid captivated by another of his stories. It wasn't a new story; we'd all heard it before at least once. We knew exactly what happened when they started running after the pig that jumped off the truck and ran into the local butchery, but we listened anyway. I hung onto every word he said, and in the long pauses in between, you could hear a penny drop as we waited patiently for him to continue. Finally, just when I was about to get restless, he continued. We sat there, listening to grandad's stories, until granny called from the kitchen to tell us that lunch was ready: Homemade bread with thick butter, ham, lettuce, tomato, and cheese. "Thank you, my wife," grandad would say as we all sat around the kitchen table, feet swinging from the chairs. "Have you told them the story about the cheese sandwich at the beach?" my granny asked. We all started screaming with excitement, "Please, grandpa! Tell the story!" He smiled knowingly. "Next time, I promise," he said as he bit into his sandwich, and we all followed suit.

I miss those days on the itchy carpet. We spent every summer with my grandparents in their small town filled with thousands of stories. We were never bored even though there was so little to do, all thanks to granny's great cooking and grandpa's stories. He made us laugh until we almost peed our pants, and as we got older and the stories got deeper, he also made us cry and hug each other. In the eyes of the world, my grandad wasn't an extremely successful man. He left school when he was fourteen to care for his family after his dad got sick. He started working at the railway and worked there until he retired. He didn't have any qualifications, but he was always the most impressive person in the room. Why? Because although he didn't have a certificate that said "Cum Laude," he was the most incredible storyteller that I've ever come across. As a kid, I never quite understood the power of storytelling until I went to another tedious work event where I had to talk to other people.

I tried my best to impress everyone, but nothing worked. I tried all of the tricks I've learned. I attempted to listen actively, use my body language, influence but not manipulate, and make small talk about proper topics, yet I got nowhere. That was until I shared a story about my childhood. I decided to tell one of my grandad's most popular stories. I recited it, word for word, just like my grandpa told it, and it worked! I kept their attention, and no one even checked their phones, but something wasn't quite right. Although I kept their attention, they didn't react the way we used to react when grandpa told his stories. I thought back to how my grandad used to tell stories; his candor, the way he would pause, the inflection and tone of his voice, his facial expressions, his gestures, and his hand movements. I realized that I hadn't used any of those tactics during my retelling. I knew storytelling was working because people were already paying more attention to me when I spoke, but I also knew that there was so much I still needed to learn. That was where my journey with storytelling truly began.

When you tell stories, you connect with people on a deeper level. You allow them to join you in your fantasy world of storytelling. You transform them from a dull event with dry sandwiches to your grandma's kitchen table filled with fresh pastries and orange juice. Connecting with people on a deeper level can be challenging, but with the proper storytelling techniques, you can seamlessly transition from small talk to deeper levels of connection. Even if you've never told a story in your life, you can be a storyteller. With the right attitude, you can turn every conversation into a captivating story moment. This chapter is all about the art of storytelling and how we can use stories to connect with and captivate an audience. We'll talk about the art of storytelling, the four types of stories you can tell at work, tips to tell a great story, how to use storytelling in your profession, and how to get other people to share their stories with you. If you're anxious about telling someone a story, take a deep breath and remember that this is not about being perfect. Telling stories is about sharing a piece of your heart with others and allowing them to do the same. It's about honesty, and it's an act of bravery. You don't have to be the perfect storyteller to tell a story. You just need to start.

## STORYTELLING AS A TOOL

Storytelling isn't magic. It's simply a tool we use to convey the one thing that connects all human beings: emotion. Emotions are at the core of all human interaction (Dolan, 2018). That's why we thrive when we have people to connect with, both personally and professionally. Storytelling is a magnificent tool to naturally include emotion in a conversation. Storytelling might not be the most obvious way to network with other professionals, but when done right, it's by far one of the most effective ways. The reason why storytelling is so effective is not "just because." There's actually a science to it.

The human brain has two separate parts, each with its own job (Dolan, 2018). The left side of your brain helps you to think logically, while the right side helps you to express emotion or recall personal memories. When we tell stories, all the parts of our brains get stimulated to work together. It combines logic, emotions, words, and sensory images. This means that stories provoke emotion, make us feel emotions, and help us to connect with others personally. In fact, a study by Paul Zak found that when we tell or listen to stories, our brains release Oxytocin, also known as the trust hormone (Dolan, 2018). Meaning when you share a story with someone, a bond of trust starts to form between you and the other person. Let's take a look at how this can influence you at work.

I have a friend, Mike, who works in sales. He struggled to make sales for a long time and was on the brink of quitting and starting a new career. That's when he started telling stories. Suddenly, his sales increased significantly, and today he is one of his company's top salesmen. Thanks to the oxytocin, the clients found that they could trust Mike, which made answering the question, "Should I buy from him?" much easier. However, if Mike didn't recognize the power of storytelling, he might still struggle to make sales today.

Take a moment and ask yourself, "How can storytelling contribute to my success?" Do you feel disconnected from your clients? Or perhaps there's no trust between you and your colleagues? Maybe you should tell your boss a story and see whether her attitude towards you changes. Even my grandfather used his storytelling as a tool. No, he didn't try to get sales or convince us of anything, but he used it as a tool to entertain us. He knew that there wasn't much else to do in their town and that if they wanted us to continue our visits, he would need a way to keep us entertained so that gran could get some things done. So he used it as a tool to connect with us, sharing stories of his childhood with us, making us feel as if we've been part of his life forever. No matter how anxious you feel, start by practicing one story. It doesn't have to be profound or funny; it just has to be yours. The more you start telling stories, the more comfortable you'll start to feel.

## THE FOUR TYPES OF STORIES

An important lesson I learned the hard way is that not all stories are work appropriate. People in different situations will react differently to your stories, and it's up to you to read the room and know what type of story would work best. The story's goal will also influence the type of story you tell. For example, when I tried convincing my boss to give me a day off on short notice, I probably shouldn't have led with the story of how I was late this morning because I overslept. Sure, earlier, my colleagues found it funny, but it wasn't the right story for the time. So let's look at four different types of stories that you can use professionally and the purpose of each story.

### *Personal Stories: To Connect*

You naturally connect with people when you share stories about your personal life. Think of a few personal stories that you can call on when you need to connect with someone. Personal stories are somewhat of an invitation for others to share their personal stories. They are great for building teams and onboarding new employees (Dolan, 2018). Now, you get personal stories, and then you get *in-your-face-you-probably-should-not-have-said-that* personal stories. Maybe stay away from incredibly emotional stories when it's the first time you're meeting someone. Funny personal stories are always a great way to start, but there's also a limit to that. Find the balance between being personal yet still appropriate. Good personal story topics include:

- pets
- family
- growing up
- home town
- school
- food

### Hypotheticals: To Encourage

Some of the best stories are yet to be written (Dolan, 2018). When you share an encouraging message, the goal is often to inspire and motivate a team toward a reality that doesn't exist yet. You want to create innovative solutions to help your team press on, even when the outcome is unclear. The best way to do this is to look at your audience and present them with characters and challenges that they need to overcome. Then, show them how they can overcome it. Finally, invite the audience to be part of the solution. For example, if your team is struggling to meet a deadline and needs to work overtime, you can share a story of how amazing it will feel tomorrow when there's no stress or overdue work.

You can tell them what you'll do with your weekend without worries and invite them to do the same.

### Case Studies: To Guide

Case studies are stories within the organization, customer stories, or industry stories you share as a guide. The goal is to tell a story where someone else has already gone through what you are currently facing, using the story as a guide on how to proceed. It doesn't have to include data and graphs, but if you have some statistics at the top of your head, feel free to share them. For example, when I started my second job, we faced a similar problem to the one I faced at my first job. So, I confidently shared how we handled the situation at my previous job, including what I think we could have done better. The story guided my new manager on how to handle the situation and prevented us from making the same mistakes as my previous company.

### Metaphors: To Persuade

If you want to persuade someone, metaphorical stories can be the perfect fit. Metaphors can be drawn from almost anything and can really persuade people to be open to something new. I have a couple of go-to metaphors that I enjoy using when I need to persuade people. I remember the one time I wanted to start a new project at work, but my boss wasn't convinced that it would be successful. He told me that the project seemed "far-fetched." Instead of giving up, I knew I had to convince him, so I asked him if he knew who the Wright brothers were. "Of course! They invented the airplane," he replied, a little confused by my question. So, I preceded by telling him that when they first started their venture, people told them that it was unrealistic, unlikely, and far-fetched. Yet, they knew they could do it, just like I knew I could handle the new project. He was quiet for a moment and then agreed that I explore the new project I had in mind.

As you can see, every story has its reason and goal. So before you start word vomiting, ask yourself what you want to achieve with this story, and choose the appropriate story that aligns with your goal.

## HOW TO TELL A GREAT STORY

When it comes to storytelling, everyone has their own way of doing it. You can add your own flavor and make it as "you" as possible, but you still need the basic ingredients. According to the experts at Harvard Business School, a great story consists of six elements, and it's essential to include all six elements to ensure that your story is balanced and well-executed (O'Hara, 2015). Of course, once you have the basics down, you can switch things up and mold them to your liking, but as someone who struggles with anxiety, it might be best to start with the basics and work your way up.

### Start With a Message

Before you jump right in and tell a story, begin by asking yourself what message you want to share with your audience (O'Hara, 2015). Your story should have a clear message in mind that guides every part of the story. Settle on your message and let it guide your storytelling. The message doesn't have to be clear to the audience from the start, but as they look back, they must think, "Aha, that makes sense!" Thinking about the message you want to convey will help you tailor the story so that you don't end up sharing irrelevant details during a 15-minute meeting.

### Mine Your Own Experience

The best stories are those that are personal to you. Use your own life experience to fuel your story (O'Hara, 2015). Allow your own memories and life experience to illustrate the message that you want to convey. Use your own failures and successes to enhance your message. We often feel reluctant to share personal information with others, but if it's an anecdote that illustrates the story's message, lean in and share it. Vulnerability can be scary, but it makes for the best storytelling (O'Hara, 2015). Remember Brené Brown, master communicator, and incredible speaker? Her whole reason for being a successful communicator was her vulnerability. So, be brave and decide to be a bit more vulnerable next time you talk with someone.

### Have a Hero

Every story needs a hero. No matter if you're simply sharing a story about a pig in a butchery or trying to convince your boss of something by using the Wright brothers as an example. Ask yourself, "Who is the hero of this story?" It's okay to make yourself the hero of the story occasionally, but be careful not to come across as the main character who can't do anything wrong. You can always be a central figure in the story, but the ultimate focus should be the lessons you've learned (O'Hara, 2015). For example, if you're welcoming new employees, make them the heroes of your story! Alternatively, if you're talking to a stakeholder, make them the hero.

### Highlight a Struggle

Imagine a movie without a struggle... it's not very interesting, is it? The same goes when telling a story. Good stories always include some sort of conflict. There needs to be a challenge for the audience to feel invested. Don't be afraid to share the difficulties you or your company has experienced. In fact, you can even lead your story by saying that the most challenging part is yet to come, but together you can face anything. Including the audience in your problem-solving will keep them engaged and invested. Highlight the struggle by embedding a rallying cry, encouraging everyone to join forces and work together (O'Hara, 2015).

### Keep It Simple

Not every story needs to be epic, filled with plot twists and complicated characters. Keep your story simple, especially if the time is short. Some stories simply require straightforward telling (O'Hara, 2015). One of the biggest mistakes people make when telling stories is putting too many details into parts of the story that don't really matter. If the message doesn't need it, lose it. You don't have to explain what you wore that day in detail if the message is actually about what you ate.

### Practice Makes Perfect

The last element of good storytelling is all about practice, practice, practice. It requires repeated effort before you can master it, so don't be discouraged if your first story doesn't go exactly as planned. Just stick with it and continue to practice the stories you have in mind. Prepare a couple of stories you can rely on, but be careful not to overuse them. Not every occasion calls for a story, but when you have it ready, you'll know when to use it (O'Hara, 2015). I suggest taking a couple of minutes a day to practice your storytelling. I like to search for a topic by using *The Story Shack* website (Just type it in on Google and you'll find loads of ideas!) and find a random topic. I then proceed to tell a five-minute story on that topic, using the skills we just discussed. The goal is to have your brain practice coming up with stories, not to already have a story ready to go! At the end of each day, take five minutes to write a story about something that happened that day and think about how you can use this in future conversations. This will allow your brain to start noticing potential stories in your everyday life, making it easier to come up with your daily story around any random topic.

## GETTING PEOPLE TO SHARE THEIR STORIES

We know that telling stories can get people to open up to you and improve relationships. So, is it safe to assume that when others tell stories, the same thing happens? Absolutely! The trick is getting others to share stories freely. Think about it as a story swap. When you tell a story, you create an opportunity for the other person to return the favor and share their own story. As wonderful and great as it sounds, there's an art to getting other people to share their stories as well.

I embarrassingly admit that it took me a while to realize that me telling stories isn't like a comedian doing stand-up. A comedian gets paid to share stories nonstop. But, if you do that in conversation, it gets a little weird (speaking out of experience). So, it's quite important to get people to share their stories with you. Luckily, I fell face first and learned the hard truths so that you don't have to (you're welcome).

Most people are cautious of following up a story with a story of their own because what if it's not as entertaining as the story just told? Or what if no one finds it interesting? So, even though they might have a story in mind, they're reluctant to share it. So, how do we get them to share it? It's quite simple: you ask. Let's say you just finished telling a story about your childhood and how life was in the small public school you went to. Once you've finished telling the story, instead of jumping in immediately with another one, take a moment and ask the other person what their experience in school was like. By asking such an open-ended question, you leave the floor open to them. Try something like this:

"I love hearing stories about when we were young and in school. How about you? Do you have any school stories you wouldn't mind sharing?"

Immediately, you let the other person know you care and want to listen. Secondly, you create a space for them to respond with a story, not just a "yes" or a "no." Most importantly, show that you're interested once they start telling their story. Remember, the more they talk, and the better you listen, the less talking you'll have to do. Practice active listening when someone is telling a story, and never interrupt their story with one of your own. It's also important not to undermine their story. Imagine you just told a great story, and then someone goes, "That's not as funny as the time I went dancing with…" Immediately you'll feel undermined and less inclined to tell another story. So, if you want to tell a story that bounces off someone else's, be sure to transition it without undermining their story. A better way to approach it would be, "Wow, that's so funny! It reminds me of the time I went dancing…" Do you see the difference? Small things like this encourage others to continue to share their stories with you.

It's good to ask people questions that get them to open up and share their experiences with you, but what happens when you ask a question, and someone starts telling a story that's offensive or inappropriate? Let's discuss taboo topics in the next chapter and how to stay confident in those awkward conversations.

# 7

## TABOO TOPICS

I used to fear accidentally offending someone the way little kids fear the Grinch on Christmas eve. I was determined never to say anything offensive, so I never spoke to anyone slightly different than me. One day, one of my colleagues walked in as I was sipping my morning coffee in the breakroom. In my head, I had a good relationship with Grace. I mean, we never spoke, but I always tried my best to be respectful. You see, growing up, I had very little interaction with the black community, and since I was so afraid of saying something offensive, I completely avoided Grace, my black female colleague. Grace was kind and lovable, and I knew she was known for her fantastic sense of humor. I assumed she was just a happy-go-lucky person and didn't even notice that I avoided her as much as possible. However, that morning in the breakroom, everything changed. As she walked in, Grace looked over at me, and I gave her my polite "I'm an introvert" smile and nod, and immediately looked away. She poured herself a cup of coffee and sat down right across from me.

"Carl, why are you scared of talking to me?" I was caught completely off guard by her openness and by the fact that she actually addressed me personally. I didn't know what to say. I started stuttering, trying to come up with an excuse. Finally, she smiled and said, "You can tell me the truth, you know. Rather speak truthfully now than live the rest of your life in regret." I smiled, took a deep breath, and told her exactly why I was scared of talking to her. "I don't want to say something and offend you. I don't want to be *that guy* that unknowingly says something against the black community or against females. Frankly, I don't know what is okay or isn't, so I just avoid the possibilities altogether." It felt strange being so honest with the woman I've been avoiding the last couple of months. I half expected her to be angry or offended, but she calmly took a sip of her coffee and said, "I respect that. Thank you for sharing your thoughts with me. How about we have more open conversations like this instead of avoiding each other?" I smiled, and we agreed that we would always be honest with each other, which gave me the freedom to talk to her without fear. Instead of being scared, I would say something wrong; I would ask her whether it was offensive or how things are usually done in the black community. I remember on one occasion, she came into the office with her hair braided in a way I'd never seen before. I walked up to her and asked, "Is it okay if I compliment your braids?" She laughed and said, "Please do!"

I think many of us are scared that we might offend others or say something that would get us in trouble. There are so many different political and social movements that we need to be aware of, all in constant arguments with each other. Now, I don't know about you, but most people with social anxiety aren't too keen on starting an office debate! So, we keep to ourselves and avoid all taboo topics. Besides, there are so many resources telling us to stay away from conversations regarding religion, race, and gender in the workspace that it's easier just to avoid them. The problem is that we can't afford to avoid having meaningful conversations with other people! Life is too short and diverse to just keep to yourself and never branch out and learn about other walks of life. In fact, when we avoid taboo conversations, we are actually more likely to say something offensive out of pure ignorance. Talking and befriending Grace made me realize that although we are different, we can still get along and work together successfully. I will forever be grateful for Grace and her courage to talk to me openly and candidly that day.

I learned a lot from Grace, especially how she navigated polarizing topics. I would love to share what I learned with you so you can also stop avoiding taboo conversations and navigate them successfully.

## TIPS FOR NAVIGATING POLARIZING TOPICS

As I researched navigating polarizing topics in the workplace, I found an article by Forbes Magazine that immediately made me think of Grace. Everything I read in the article regarding navigating conversations was exactly how Grace managed our situation, and it's how I've been trying to navigate situations since. So let's have a look.

### *Respectful Dialogue*

Instead of avoiding dialogue, the goal should be to facilitate respectful dialogue. Not all work environments have a culture where open dialogue is welcome, but that doesn't mean you can't have meaningful conversations. Showing respect in conversation is about listening, seeing their point of view, and not forcing your own ideas onto the other person. If you don't agree with a statement, be sure to state that you disagree with their statement and not with them as a person. Avoid making assumptions about a person based on their looks and acknowledge your common ground. Grace was always respectful in our conversations and never looked down on me for not knowing things about her culture. Instead of laughing at me or "canceling" me because of my ignorance, she was kind and helpful. In the same way, I showed respect by not looking down on her culture when there are things that are done differently in my culture. No matter whom you talk to or how different you are, you can always be respectful of other people (Forbes, 2021).

### *Define Expectations*

Knowing what to expect is a saving grace to anyone with anxiety. After my conversation with Grace, I knew exactly what to expect in our conversations. We both agreed on being honest, open, and respectful even when we disagreed. We also gave each other permission to kindly correct the other when we did something inappropriate, and it was such a relief to know that someone had my back. Before addressing a polarizing topic, set some expectations. Agree on being respectful and communicating calmly. It's also important to communicate that expectation to others as well. For example, I was working with another man on a project once who made an incredibly sexist joke. Even though there weren't any women around, I knew that being

sexist was not something I wanted to add to my reper-
toire, so I communicated kindly to him that when he
worked with me, there would be none of that. I set the
expectation for him, and he never made another sexist
comment in the office again.

### Treat Everyone With Kindness

The best way to handle polarizing topics is with kindness and empathy. Instead of seeing the problem you
have with the person, take a moment and think about
them personally. Think about all their hardships, and
go into the conversation with empathy and kindness
towards the person (Forbes, 2021). Instead of judgment,
be intentional with your understanding, even when a
colleague has done something wrong. When you
approach every topic with kindness and empathy, the
chances of it blowing up and turning into a heated
argument are significantly less.

### Educate Yourself

When things blow up and people get heat for doing
something inappropriate, they'll say, "I didn't know." As
true as it might be, there comes a point when you must
stop using ignorance as an excuse and educate yourself
on polarizing topics. For example, if someone starts
working with you and they're religious, take a couple of
minutes and educate yourself on that religion. I'm not

saying you should know EVERYTHING, but knowing something might help you to navigate difficult conversations better. If you really want to, you can always do a short online course about diversity or ask your colleague to teach you some things about their religion or culture. Chances are that if you ask them for help educating you, they'll be more tolerant when you get something wrong because they know you're trying.

### *Have Constructive Conversations*

When you don't agree with someone, especially regarding a taboo topic, it can quickly become a heated debate and get blown out of proportion. The goal is to have constructive conversations instead of heated arguments. When you disagree with someone, or you can feel there's tension, do what Grace did: Approach them with kindness in a space where you can talk freely, ask them what the problem is, and work together to find a solution for the issue. Discussing the problem openly with the other person will also prevent office gossip from spreading, and if you work together to find a solution, it will strengthen your work relationship (Forbes, 2021).

By applying these five tips in polarizing conversation, you'll find the confidence to engage with everyone and discuss matters of importance with other individuals. The goal is to expand your perspective to be more inclusive and aware. So let's look at how we can expand our perspective of others more.

## EXPAND YOUR PERSPECTIVE OF OTHERS

Expanding your perspective of others isn't hard in itself, but it takes some work in order for you to change your way of thinking. However, even the slightest change can help you to lead better, make better decisions, and influence your colleagues positively. Here are five ways in which you can expand your perspective of others:

### Listen More

We've touched on this point multiple times earlier in the book, but I literally can't stress this enough. Listening to others is so incredibly important when you're in conversation with someone. Listen not just to what they are saying but to how they view the world and interpret certain situations. This will help you to change your perspective of them in the future (Eikenberry, 2013).

### Spend Time Together

The more time you spend with people, the better you'll understand them and how they think. Spending a lot of time with people from different communities, cultures, and religions will broaden your perspective on the world and help you feel less intimidated the next time you're conversing with someone new (Eikenberry, 2013).

### Ask Questions

Instead of assuming you know what someone believes, ask them a question. Be open to hearing their perspective and allow it to broaden your view on life. The more questions you ask, the more you'll know about the other person, their views, and what they believe in (Eikenberry, 2013). Don't be scared to ask difficult questions. Good questions can lead to great conversation and a better understanding of each other.

### Look Through Different Filters

Try to look at the world through different lenses, not just your own bias. Try to remove yourself from the picture and imagine what it is like for the other person. This will help you to be more understanding and open to hearing how they experience something. Remember, just because something doesn't bother or offend you doesn't mean it won't bother or offend someone else. Be open to others' experiences by imagining it from inside their shoes.

Now that you have a better understanding of how to deal with difficult topics, we'll take it a step further in the next chapter and discuss how we can deal with difficult people. Yes, I know someone's name just popped into your head! That's okay, though. Not everyone is easy to work with, but with the right tools, it can be possible to talk to literally anyone, even the crazies.

# 8

## THE CRAZIES

You can be the best smooth talker in the world, with zero social anxiety and all the social skills out there, and you'll still run into people you don't get along with. That is the beauty and chaos of living in a world where we are all so different. Usually, when this happens, there's some kind of conflict. In some cases, there's an explosion when two people who don't get along have finally had enough of each other, and... BOOM! In other cases, conflict is more subtle. You start avoiding each other, whisper behind each other's backs, and roll your eyes whenever they say, well, anything. When you work with a lot of other people, it's bound to happen that; eventually, you'll run into someone you do not get along with. I'm sure you can think of someone right now that you've worked with at some point in your life. Let me tell you the story of my friend Ryann.

Ryann had worked at an advertising agency for about two years when she met her new colleague, Emma. Although Emma was new to Ryann, she wasn't new to the company. She was one of the first employees that started at the agency but took a two-year break to pursue her master's degree. Emma was extremely hard-working, which Ryann admired, yet there was something that just didn't click. You see, while Emma was gone, Ryann was tasked to pick up a lot of the things that Emma used to do, but the moment Emma got back, she reclaimed all her roles and projects, leaving Ryann feeling like a third wheel on Valentine's Day. Ryann tried her best to get along with Emma, but she was constantly silenced, given tasks that no one wanted to do, and basically played "intern" to Emma. When Ryann addressed the issue with her manager, she realized that Emma was the golden child who could do no wrong since she's been with the company from the start. Ryann decided that she wanted to clear the air, so she and Emma went out for breakfast one morning. The two women started talking, and Ryann could share a lot of things with Emma vulnerably. They both realized just how different they were, but they were able to address some of the issues they had with one another openly, calmly, and without too much drama. Since then, they've had an agreement: We don't have to invite each other over for coffee and pretend like we're besties, but at work, we'll have each other's backs and respect one another.

Do the two women now always get along? Of course not! But do they have a system when things go wrong? Absolutely. Even though it took Ryann to admit that she would quit if things didn't get better, eventually, they could put their conflict aside and make the best out of a difficult situation. In this chapter, we'll talk more about dealing with conflict and how you can deal with even the most difficult people in the world (which is definitely that person you thought of earlier). So let's have a look!

## DEALING WITH CONFLICT

The first thing to notice when dealing with conflict at work is that it's very different from dealing with conflict at home. Although it's definitely not advised, when dealing with conflict at home, it's okay if you occasionally slam a door shut or say something like, "You make me crazy!" However, despite what reality tv might teach us when you're at work, you always need to remain professional. So, let's talk through the steps of dealing with conflict (Blink, 2018):

1. **Talk to the other person.** This is not the time to play the quiet, passive-aggressive game where you leave it for as long as possible until the other person notices something's up by the way you slam your stapler. Instead, approach the person and ask them when would be a good time to chat and arrange a setup where you won't be interrupted by others.

2. **Address the behavior and not the person.** Refrain from pointing out all of their flaws and annoying mannerisms, and rather address a specific behavior that bothered you. Describe the instance rather than making it a generalized action.

3. **Listen carefully.** Don't get into attack mode, but listen to what the person is saying. Ask questions to clarify what they are saying, and don't interrupt them when they're trying to explain the situation from their perspective.

4. **Identify points of disagreement.** Communicate what it is you agree on and what it is that you're disagreeing on. Ask the other person whether they agree with your analysis of what you agree and disagree on.

5. **Develop a plan.** Once you've agreed on the problem, ask for recommendations on how to deal with it. Then, work together to find a

midway and be willing to compromise on some things.

6. **Follow through.** It's one thing to have a plan and another to follow through. Stick to what you have agreed on and decide to give the other person the benefit of the doubt going forward.

Now that you have some steps to deal with conflict, it's up to you to do something about it. I know it can be daunting, but the quicker you address the problem, the less anxiety it will cause in your life. So frequently, we leave things for later, but the more you leave it, the more the anxiety brews within you, playing out scenarios that are so far-fetched that it puts you into flight mode. Rather address it quickly and calmly and then move on.

## DEALING WITH GOSSIP

Dealing with conflict is one thing, but dealing with gossip requires a whole other game plan. As perfect and great as your workspace might be, gossip will always be part of any organization. Although gossip isn't all bad since it signifies colleagues that are open and close to one another, it can quickly become toxic and make any work environment terrible. But what can you do if you're being approached with juicy gossip about what

Susan saw on Betty's Instagram this weekend? How do you spot and avoid gossip without being an outcast? Well, it's easy to spot gossip when you know what to look for. Here are a few things you can look out for when you're unsure whether it's just weekend chitchat or gossip.

1. **Tone of voice:** When someone's talking to you in their normal voice, it's probably not gossip. Usually, when they start whispering or lowering their voice so only you can hear what they're saying, they're telling you a secret or gossiping. If what they're saying is about themselves, you're in the clear, but if they're discussing someone else in a lowered voice, it's gossip (Cooks-Campbell, 2022). There's a very thin line between "venting" and gossiping. It's okay to vent every now and then, but if the venting becomes a personal attack on someone, cut it off.

2. **No clear source:** Gossip usually doesn't have a clear source. When there's suddenly whispers about layoffs or unethical behaviors, unpleasant stories start popping up everywhere. It's hard to pinpoint where gossip started, and you'll probably get stonewalled when you try to find the source. If someone tells you that they heard

something from someone who saw something at the mall two months ago, it's safe to assume it's gossip.

3. **The topic of conversation:** With gossip, the person you're talking about is usually not present. If you're unsure whether something is gossip, ask yourself whether this person would repeat what they just said in front of the person you're discussing. Cut it off if the answer is no (Cooks-Campbell, 2022).

As easy as it is to say, "just cut it off," it can be hard to do so, especially if you have social anxiety. For example, I used to hate it when people came to me with office gossip, but I felt so included and relieved that people were talking to me and not I to them that I would just keep quiet and nod. The problem is, I pretty soon became the office gossip without ever saying a word because everyone knew I wouldn't tell anyone else or oppose what they're saying. So, when I finally found my confidence and began my journey of improving my anxiety and communication, I realized that I had to do something about it. Here's what I did:

1. If someone came to me and started gossiping, I would say something positive about the person they were discussing. As strange as it might

sound, positive gossip is real and can be very powerful in changing perspectives.

2. I would set boundaries. As soon as I recognized gossip, I would call it out and ask that the other person didn't include me in the gossip. Calling out the gossip doesn't have to be extremely awkward, like, "That's gossip; I don't appreciate it when you gossip about other people." That is the quickest way to send you into being outcasted from any and all future conversations, which is definitely not what we want. However, you can say, "I would really appreciate it if you didn't talk that way about [Ellen]. She is not here to defend herself, and I don't like to talk about people behind their backs." Then, you can change the subject and ask them about their own life. Many times people don't even realize that they are "gossiping" about someone else, so you saying this line to them can help them realize that maybe they weren't saying the most respectful things and that if the person were there in the room, would they still be talking that way.

3. Finally, I made sure that space was created to speak freely about feelings outside the workspace. For example, if someone wanted to come to me and vent, I would suggest that we

grab a coffee or lunch and discuss it, in which I would then encourage them to have a conversation with the person they're gossiping about.

Cutting off gossip might be awkward the first few times, but the message will soon spread that you're not interested in harmful conversations, and people will actually appreciate and respect you for it. Because just think about it. We all know that office gossip or someone who just talks badly about everyone else when they aren't around. It makes you think... *"If they are talking badly about everyone else...what are they saying about me..."* However, when you become known as that person who doesn't entertain gossip and will actively shut it down, people will begin to feel safer around you. They will feel safe knowing that you aren't talking behind their back about them and that you aren't listening to the gossip that comes through the social channels.

## DEALING WITH YOUR BOSS

Dealing with colleagues and conflict is one thing, but what if you have a conflict with your boss? You have two options: resign, pack your bags, change your name, and flee the country, or you could talk about it. I know the first option sounds more appealing than the second for anyone with social anxiety, but I promise you, the second option makes more sense. When you need to talk to your boss regarding something they did or said or to resolve a conflict between the two of you, there are a few things that you can do to make the process less painful (Smith, 2013):

1. Think about the situation before you approach your boss. Know what you want to say and rehearse it a little bit if you have to. Be prepared to receive pushback and know what you want from the conversation.

2. Calculate the risk and know what you're putting on the line. Approach the conversation with respect even if you feel like your boss doesn't deserve it.

3. Make sure you pick the right time to approach your boss. If it's right before an important meeting, don't do it. Rather schedule a meeting with your boss so that you both know when the conversation will happen and can prepare accordingly.

4. Be professional and don't fall into "he said, she said" scenarios. At the end of the day, they're still your boss and are paying you for a service. Remember to give it time since not all conflict

is resolved immediately, but be sure that you keep your side of the street clean.

5. Don't involve all your colleagues with the hopes of starting a "mob mentality" against your boss. Someone will tell them about it, and then you can say goodbye to any chance of resolving the conflict without collateral damage.

There you have it! Now you can approach and embrace conflict with ease. Remember that conflict isn't always a bad thing. In fact, usually, after conflict, the relationship grows faster and more robust. When conflict is done right, it can boost relationships correctly. If it's awkward to approach someone and discuss the conflict between you, do it anyway. It's okay not always to be the smoothest talker or the coolest person in the room. Just remember your communication tools, use them effectively, and be yourself.

# CONCLUSION

I recently met a woman who is radiating success and interest. She's confident and successful. Her smile never falters, yet everyone takes her seriously. She is friendly, yet the whole world stops and listens when she speaks. She is kind yet strong. Moreover, even though she runs the show and demands to be taken seriously, she is still well-liked and seems to get along with everyone. No, I'm not talking about Karen, our Little Miss Perfect.

I'm talking about you!

Perhaps you're not feeling any different than you did 30 000 words ago, but you are. Do you know why? Because you're equipped. That unfair advantage that everyone else seems to have is now yours! You have all the tools in your utility belt, ready to face whatever

## 160 | CONCLUSION

social situation may come your way. No, your anxiety didn't magically disappear, and no, everyone isn't going to automatically love you the moment you walk into the room, but you'll get there. If you're not convinced, just take a moment and think about all the things you've learned on this journey:

- You've learned the importance of communication and how to use it to your advantage instead of feeling like you're at a disadvantage.
- You've learned how to make a killer first impression, and that spilling wine on yourself before you meet the parents is probably not a good move (thanks for the lesson, Jason).
- You've learned how to remain confident in every situation and are now equipped with the right tools to find your calm when you need it.
- You've mastered small talk, know which topics to avoid, and know how to ask the right questions to get people talking.
- You've learned how to build relationships with authenticity and not through manipulation.
- You've unlocked the power of storytelling and all the wonderful things that go with it.
- You've learned to embrace polarizing conversations and approach them with respect.

- You finally know how to deal with THAT guy. You can confidently handle the Brads and the Karens of this world, knowing that you are equipped to deal with anyone, even the crazies.

Above all, I hope you've learned to embrace who you are and not hide yourself away because of social anxiety. You, my slightly awkward friend, are magnificent! You have everything in you to make your life a success, communicate confidently, and take the proper steps toward your future. It's been incredible to take this journey with you, and I know this is only the beginning for you. I can't wait to hear your success story and get inspired by your confidence. I hope this journey has been as incredible for you as it has been for me.

You are a force to be reckoned with, and whenever you think you can't do it, do it anyway. Who knows, you might surprise yourself and do what once seemed impossible, like starting a global podcast...

(Oh, one last bit of advice. If all else fails, just talk about puppies. People love dogs, so just go with it)!

YOUR FREE GIFT!

As a thank you for purchasing my book, I would love to give you a free gift! This book is chock-full of everything you need to talk to anyone at work, but for all the recovering awkwards out there, it extends way beyond just work. Don't miss out on this list of the best resources for you along your journey to becoming *recovered* awkward person.

https://bit.ly/resources4awkwards

COULD YOU HELP ME TO HELP MORE PEOPLE?

If you're anything like me, as soon as you feel the changes in yourself, you're going to want to spread the word and help other awkward people like us... and you can!

Simply by sharing your honest opinion of this book on Amazon, you'll show new readers where they can find all the tools they need to improve their confidence and feel comfortable in their own skin.

Thank you so much for your support. We all deserve to feel comfortable in ourselves... and together, we can make sure more people do.

Just scan the QR code on the next page to leave your review.

# REFERENCES

American Psychological Association. (2022). *Mindfulness*. American Psychological Association. https://www.apa.org/topics/mindful ness#:~:text=Mindfulness%20is%20awareness%20of%20one

Attia, P. [Peter Attia MD]. (2022, December 26). *Advantages of creating systems and not just setting goals*. YouTube. https://youtu.be/ROV36xBFD20

Blink. (2018). *How to Handle Conflict in the Workplace*. UC San Diego. https://blink.ucsd.edu/HR/supervising/conflict/handle.html#1.-Talk-with-the-other-person.

Boynton, E. (2021, September 10). *How to Practice Positive Affirmations — and Why They Work*. Right as Rain by UW Medicine. https://righ tasrain.uwmedicine.org/mind/well-being/positive-affirmations#:~:text=They%20help%20disrupt%20negative%20thought

Buchert, S., Laws, E. L., Apperson, J. M., & Bregman, N. J. (2008). *First impressions and professor reputation: influence on student evaluations of instruction*. SpringerLink. https://doi.org/10.1007/s11218-008-9055-1

Carnegie, D. (1913). *How to win friends [and] influence people*. The World's Work.

Altman, B. [Charisma on Command]. (2017, December 25). *4 Easy Ways To Make Small Talk With People* YouTube. https://www.youtube.com/watch?v=xmx07H3sn1w&ab_channel=CharismaonCommand

Clarkson, C. (2020, May 25). *How to Influence People Without Being Manipulative: Quicksilver*. MarketScale. https://marketscale.com/industries/education-technology/how-to-influence-people-with out-being-manipulative-quicksilver/

## 166 | REFERENCES

CLIMB Professional Development and Training. (2019). *The 7 Benefits of Effective Communication in Personal and Professional Settings.* Portland Community College. http://climb.pcc.edu/blog/the-7-bene fits-of-effective-communication-in-personal-and-professional-settings

Cooks-Campbell, A. (2022, August 25). *How to handle gossip in the workplace and encourage communication.* BetterUp. https://www.betterup. com/blog/gossip-in-the-workplace#:~:text=The%20negative% 20consequences%20of%20workplace%20gossip&text=Rumors% 20can%20strain%20trust%20between

Cuncic, A. (2022, February 14). *Small Talk Topics: The Best and Worst Things to Talk About.* Verywell Mind. https://www.verywellmind. com/small-talk-topics-3024421

Dolan, G. (2018, March 28). *Using stories to build and strengthen connections.* LBD Group. https://thelbdgroup.com.au/using-stories-to-build-and-strengthen-connections/

Eikenberry, K. (2013, August 26). *Six Ways to Expand Your Perspective.* The Kevin Eikenberry Group. https://kevineikenberry.com/leader ship/six-ways-to-expand-your-perspective/

Forbes. (2021, July 22). *15 Tips For Navigating Potentially Polarizing Discussions At Work.* Forbes. https://www.forbes.com/sites/ forbeshumanresourcescouncil/2021/07/22/15-tips-for-navigat ing-potentially-polarizing-discussions-at-work/?sh=7b7b6fd47a4d

Genard, G. (2019, September 2). *The Breathing Technique that Will Boost Your Confidence.* The Genard Method https://www.genardmethod. com/blog/the-breathing-technique-that-will-boost-your-confidence

Headspace. (2022). *How to stop negative self-talk.* Headspace https:// www.headspace.com/mindfulness/stop-negative-self-talk

Indeed Editorial Team. (2021, February 23). *10 Benefits of Effective Communication in the Workplace.* Indeed Career Guide. https://www. indeed.com/career-advice/career-development/communication-benefits

Jolles, R. (2020, February 25). *6 Keys to Influencing People, Not Manipulating Them*. ZenBusiness. https://www.zenbusiness.com/blog/influence-people/

Lund, P. (2021, July 7). *How To Be Your Best At Your Worst*. Forces of Equal. https://forcesofequal.com/advice/how-to-be-your-best-at-your-worst/

O'Hara, C. (2015, August 12). *How to Tell a Great Story*. Harvard Business Review. https://hbr.org/2014/07/how-to-tell-a-great-story

Olivia. (2020, October 29). *Do You Have the Right Mindset for Small Talk?* Medium. https://curiousmindproject.medium.com/the-right-mindset-for-small-talk-f20f0413a854

Psychology Today. (2011). *First Impressions*. Psychology Today https://www.psychologytoday.com/us/basics/first-impressions

*Pulsifer, C., & Gillison, B. (n.d.). 57 quotes about helping others. Inspirational Words of Wisdom. https://www.wow4u.com/helping/*

Roberts, E. (2013, March 13). *Mindfulness Can Increase Self-Confidence*. HealthyPlace https://www.healthyplace.com/blogs/buildingselfesteem/2013/03/how-mindfulness-can-increase-self-confidence

Scott, E. (2022, May 24). *The Toxic Effects of Negative Self-Talk*. Verywell Mind. https://www.verywellmind.com/negative-self-talk-and-how-it-affects-us-4161304

Shatz, I. (2022). *The Benjamin Franklin Effect: Build Rapport by Asking for Favors*. Effectiviology. https://effectiviology.com/benjamin-franklin-effect/

Slack. (2019, June 13). *4 powerful examples of effective leadership communication*. Slack. https://slack.com/blog/collaboration/effective-leadership-communication-examples

Smith, J. (2013, April 25). *How To Approach The Boss When Conflict Arises At Work*. Forbes. https://www.forbes.com/sites/jacquelynsmith/2013/04/25/how-to-approach-the-boss-when-conflict-arises-at-work/?sh=29ffd3563bd6

Stanford University. (2007, February 25). *Why Do Humans And Primates Get More Stress-related Diseases Than Other Animals?* ScienceDaily. https://www.sciencedaily.com/releases/2007/02/070218134333.htm

Star, K. (2019). *Using Visualization Techniques to Reduce Anxiety Symptoms*. Verywell Mind. https://www.verywellmind.com/visual ization-for-relaxation-2584112

*Study shows how taking short breaks may help our brains learn new skills. (2021, June 8). National Institutes of Health (NIH). https://www.nih.gov/ news-events/news-releases/study-shows-how-taking-short-breaks-may-help-our-brains-learn-new-skills*

Waters, S. (2021, December 6). *Make a good first impression: Expert tips for showing up at your best*. BetterUp. https://www.betterup.com/ blog/how-to-make-a-good-first-impression

Waters, S. (2022, May 3). *Why building great work relationships is more than just getting along*. BetterUp https://www.betterup.com/blog/ building-good-work-relationships

Weverbergh, R., & Vermoesen, K. (2022). *CEO communication: strategy and best practices*. FINN. https://www.finn.agency/ceo-communication/